THE CHOSEN SPIRIT

THE CHOSEN SPIRIT

Lawrence James

FANTINE PRESS

First published 2008
by
FANTINE PRESS
The Coach House
Stansted Hall
Stansted
Essex CM24 8UD

British Library CIP Data:
A catalogue record of this book is
available from the British Library.

ISBN 978 1 901958 20 1

Printed in England by Booksprint

ACKNOWLEDGEMENTS

There are many to thank for their valuable contributions to and help with this book.

Firstly, I would especially like to thank my very dear mother, Lilian, for without her there would be no book.

I would also like to thank my dear friend Wilf, whose wonderful gift made this book possible.

Very special thanks to all of the many spirits who have so actively and willingly contributed to this work.

My sincere thanks to Jeanette Truscott and my daughter Phillipa for their very valuable contributions.

Last, but not least, thanks must go to my old friend Dick Richards MD, for his editing, co-ordination and expert help in guiding this book towards publication.

Please remember throughout that although I am the author, it is very important to recognise that this really is my mother's book. It is she who was – and is – the fundamental key to the entire spirit connection. It is Lilian James who is truly 'The Chosen Spirit.'

L. James

CONTENTS

INTRODUCTION

If life's experiences have taught me anything useful, then one of the things I have learned is that people often make up their minds on the grounds of all too little reliable evidence. They then make things worse by refusing to be influenced by facts. Maybe they are just too lazy. Perhaps they are not open-minded enough to think again.

Well, this might be a good time to do just that, for here coming straight at you are many strange thoughts and new ideas. Some may surprise or even offend to start with, but read on and see if at least some part of their basic sense reaches you.

If it does, then prepare to have some of your old ideas shattered. Prepare to see the so-called truths of years ago demolished because here, for the first time in history, the right circumstances have come together and led to information never told to man before. It means sweeping re-appraisals and new interpretations of the Bible, the Gospels, the life and times of Jesus of Nazareth and his family, and many of today's other most puzzling problems.

All of this is because information has come to us direct from the spirit world. Whether at first you believe it or not, this has to be amongst the most astonishing material you have ever seen. For example:

9

Was Jesus Christ the physical son of God? – No.
Was Mary a virgin at the time of Jesus' conception?
  – No.
Did Jesus ever wear a crown of thorns? – No.
Was he nailed up on a cross? – No.
Did Judas Iscariot really betray Jesus? – No.
Did the living Jesus Christ rise from the dead?
  – No.
Is there a God? – Yes.
Is there a life hereafter? – Yes.
Does reincarnation happen? – Yes.
Where was – or is – Jesus buried?
Who, what and where is the being called God?
Is there really only one God?
Are we made in God's image?
Does anyone listen to our prayers?
Is there a heaven? If so, where?
Does the Devil exist?
Noah's Ark – what's the truth?
Do aliens visit the earth?
What is the problem with the Bermuda Triangle?
What really happened to the Ark of the Covenant?
Where is Atlantis?
Are there such things as UFOs?
Diana of Wales and Dodi Fayed – just how did they
die?

This list represents just a fraction of the well over
three hundred questions asked, and answers
supplied, in this book.

At times – and to some it seems as if this book came
about my accident or pure coincidence. As time has
passed, however, both the scientifically trained and
the more spiritually minded amongst us have begun
to wonder if it was a matter of coincidence after all.

Could it not really have been a project influenced by non-human agencies? This is a question likely to arise in the mind of every reader. Each must decide this for him or herself.

This book's editor, my friend of many years, is, so far, a life-long atheist. Working on this book has made even him feel doubts. For him, new and unexpected explanations have arisen. Foremost amongst these, he says, has been the claim that there really is a God, albeit that He is not by any means the caring God Almighty of the Bible. Far from it. Next, comes the denial of the idea that Jesus was the physical son of a god. So is the idea that Jesus' body was physically resurrected from the grave after his death.

For Jesus, as we shall hear claimed, was the illegitimate son of a servant girl, Mary. He had no miraculous birth with shepherds or stars in the East. He seldom moved from Jerusalem, where he was born, lived and died. Jesus never lived in Nazareth and never performed miracles.

Before ending this introduction, I would like to outline the main pattern of the book and the events related. This is in the hope that it will help avoid confusion arising from the book's questions and answers which, though edited into main sections, remain largely as spontaneously asked and answered.

The spirit contacts state that in the beginning, a god, whom we know as God, came here from elsewhere in the universe together with his attendant heavenly spirits. On this planet, Earth, he began to experiment and raise other spirits by means of a lengthy plant and animal evolution. This culminated in humans. Now His sole concern is the developing of more spirits and He is not involved in any other way.

When humans die, they become earth spirits, children of God, and move to Heaven, where they then live happily and forever, and have as their duties the caring for their descendants still on Earth. It is sure that reincarnation happens in certain circumstances: it is certain that we will again meet our erstwhile loved ones in Heaven and stay with them always. This is the message of comfort the book hopes to offer on behalf of its guiding spirits.

Finally, I ask readers to note that much of this book is transcribed exactly as Lilian James' words came from the clairvoyant's lips and, sometimes, onto the tape recorder. Apart from editing, almost nowhere have they been significantly altered. Nowhere has their actual message been changed.

This means however, that there are occasional unexpected alterations of tense, pronoun use and emphasis much as might be expected from such a speaker and under these high-pressure conditions. There are also episodes of repetition largely where the answers to questions overlap.

Although Lilian was relating the answers as they came to her, it is clear that as she did not possess previous or well-informed knowledge of many things in the subject matter, she did not always understand the details of what she was speaking. Lilian merely reported and passed things on as they were for her or were told to her. The 'contact periods' were for her and the others involved times of great concentration and excitement. Please read on with due forbearance and with these factors kept in mind.

One thing only do I request and recommend as author – please readers, before you kill the messenger, consider the message.

Chapter 1

GOD AND RELIGION
Some Surprising Truths

Where, originally, did God and the planet Earth come from?

We are told that God originates from far out on the other side of the universe. The planet which we have named Earth slowed down while circling a sun and fell out of orbit some sixty billion years ago. It travelled for millions of miles and billions of years and finally settled here. God and His already existing family of spirits came with it. So as not to mix them up with 'earth' or 'human' spirits, I [Lilian] have called these 'heavenly spirits.'

I need to stress that God is a powerful thought and energy source. He is a cosmic spirit of His own kind. However, He is not the 'creator' of the entire universe and is certainly not the all-powerful and unpredictable 'God' of Biblical and religious beliefs and stories. There are definite limits even to His abilities. He is, in every way, a natural god. He is not supernatural and does not do supernatural things. That must be understood, as it is part of the way we have to understand everything else.

I must also stress that, for want of a better word, we refer to the place where spirits live as 'Heaven.' It is not in any way the traditional Heaven we think of as full of dead people and angels dressed in flowing, white robes gathered around some celestial throne. It is simply another universe, invisible to you – a spirit world existing right here and now, all around us. I'll try to explain as we go on doing this book.

Because of the different atmosphere, God found He could not multiply His heavenly spirits here on earth. Instead, He set about, by trial and error, to form new spiritual children. By that, I mean humans with human spirits. He developed the small plants and the simple life forms, the fish and other marine creatures, and by trial and error developed the animal kingdom. Everything gradually evolved, progressing eventually to the monkeys and gorillas and suchlike, and finally to man.

This answers one basic question you asked me. We do resemble God. That is we are in His image, but not while we are terrestrial humans living our lives on Earth. We are only in His image when we enter the spiritual kingdom and become one of His spiritual children.

What was God's first task in order to develop what is now our advanced civilisation and His new spiritual family in heaven?

Firstly, He had to create spirits of His own kind. At the beginning, He created the oceans, then the fish and the animals that left the sea and were able to breathe. Over time, He used lesser animals to eventually develop human beings to be His own spiritual children. This was all done by a process of trial and error.

A question that has puzzled man for centuries is how God started life off on this planet and there are many theories about that. Are you able to give a full answer to this question?

To start life on the Earth, God used the moon and created the tides, then showered the seashores with particles of seed energy in the form of a grey ash from Himself. He then waited and watched for the appearance of life and hoped that the development and progression of that early life would lead towards Him achieving his goal of more and more spiritual children.

We are told that God made us in His own image. How can this be as our bodies are obviously not designed to leave this planet without protection?

When God came here with His planet and found that He could not multiply his heavenly spirits on the surface, He had to develop an animal kingdom first. We are the end result, but, as yet, we are neither in His likeness nor are we one of God's earthly spirits. This does not happen until our physical body expires and our spirit is accepted into Heaven. Then, and only then, are we in His image, which is not like a human, but is as a global-shaped energy form.

It has always been told to us that the Almighty God is the God of all creation – the heavens, the earth and the universe, everything. Does the spirit world have the answer to this question?

There is one god for every planet that is inhabited. They are all gods, but we just call ours 'God.' There is only one of Him. Our God started life off on the planet called Earth. This was at the shore lines, which

He seeded directly with his energy. God overseas the planet, but everything else is monitored on a day-to-day basis by His heavenly spirits.

We earth spirits can communicate with heavenly spirits and they can connect with God, though not with speech. With Him, there is no conversation as there is between us or, sometimes, between us and you humans. God and His heavenly spirits are pure energy. They do not use language as we do.

We have spoken about God controlling this planet, but does He also have any control over the universe?

No, He controls only this planet. The earth is His planet and always has been. The other planets have their own gods, but their children are just spirits. They are not born of the flesh. Their gods do not have to supply food in the human and animal sense to support them through their development from an animal life and then on into the spiritual world.

Can God travel to meet with other gods?

God could, but He does not do so. He wants to stay here to look after his planet, His own family of spirits that He brought with Him and us, the family of earth spirits He created in His image as a candlelight-shaped globe of energy.

Why does God not actually visit planet Earth?

He is neither involved and nor is He needed. God regards his world as being perfectly in order as far as He is concerned. The earth does not need God's intervention, so He does not offer it or intrude at all. Additionally, He needs to be sustained by the energy in the upper atmosphere to continue here. Also, He is too big to come down here to Earth.

What is God's actual role now?

God is responsible for maintaining the world both physically and spiritually by supplying His energy to sustain life. He leaves the tasks and responsibilities of looking after you to us spirits and we do this mostly on a family basis. Each of us looks after members of our earth families who are still living on Earth.

When did God build the energy tunnels?

At the point when God realised He had almost achieved his dream of creating an animal-human spirit worthy of coming into His spiritual kingdom of heaven. He wanted all spirits to be able to move about the planet and the heavens quickly, so He made these sort of tunnels. We move in them without seeming to move at all yet we get from one place to another just the same and very rapidly.

How many Gods are there?

There is a god on every star and nearly all of the planets. This planet belongs to our God. There are no other gods here.

What is God's relationship with the sun and moon?

He relies on the sun for heat and light, and uses the moon partially to influence the weather systems and the tides.

How does God maintain His energy?

He draws strength from the sun's energy and from the atmosphere and then pushes His energy down to supply the heavenly spirits as well as pushing energy further down to us earthly spirits. Without the sun, we would not have any energy and would not be able to survive. God is of the sun and depends on it like we do.

Does God have emotions?

He only has peace and love for us, and especially when we arrive into the spirit world.

Why does God, who went to all the trouble to create us, allow us to suffer the pain and traumas that we have to endure throughout our lives? Why does He seem to do nothing about it?

It is not a question of God allowing suffering. It is just that He is not directly involved in our lives in this way or at this level at all.

In the beginning, God spread a form of ash about the shores of the earth. God and His spirits constantly monitored and guided the course of evolution, and the development of new species and the phasing out of others that were less successful. When mankind, the first truly intelligent species, evolved, God ceased to be involved in the small events of their lives. All animals now have to fend for themselves and survive on the planet's surface.

God's heavenly spirits tried to control this, but the animals tried to inter-breed and nothing became of it. Whatever happens to us in the animal kingdom and throughout our lives is mere chance, the fortune or misfortune of incidental events that affect us for good or bad. God has no place in any of this. It is not a matter for His concern. He has other things to attend to.

God had to create a sustainable food chain from the seas to the land and to work through the evolution of the animal kingdom to develop His spiritual children. It is an essential part of life in this animal kingdom that pain and survival are closely linked.

We, the earth spirits, with our limited abilities try to help you with the problems this causes. But you are there to develop and reproduce according to the events that befall you and your own individual abilities. When you finally come to Heaven and become one of His children, that is when He looks after you. It may be seen as unfortunate that we all have to face what ordeals come our way on our way to Heaven, but neither God nor we spirits have any other choice.

God has produced enough food, the trees, plants and animals for everyone. If you all decided to work together instead of competing, then the food could be shared fairly and would be sufficient.

With regard to illness, if you decide to eat the wrong foods, it is your fault. All the cures for illness are there: they just have to be found and used. Society is not working the way it should. I see that all very clearly now. There is much too much greed when there should be a lot more co-operation, compassion and help towards the needy and less fortunate.

Now that we know God does not listen or heed our individual problems or needs, may we ask does He have any opinions or care directly about us in His human/animal and spiritual kingdom?

He loves his planet and He is proud of what He has achieved. He has finally formed the level of new spiritual family that He was trying to achieve. Now that He has succeeded, He is just monitoring us while He considers His next step. If He ever decides that He must leave, He will take us all with him.

Do angels exist and if so do they have wings?

Yes, angels do exist, but they do not have wings. The angels are usually chosen from young spirits who have passed over prematurely. They have much more energy than us because of their youth. They can achieve so much more. Some spirits are also chosen to be angels in order to do special deeds or duties.

With regards to religion, is it practised or taught in the spirit world?

There is no religion as you know it on earth. We are all equal and children of God. There are no conflicts of ideas and beliefs. These are all just silly human ideas and are not important here.

What role does religion play for both mankind and in our various communities around the world?

Religions play a role in communities as part of a way of life. Different religions believe in different gods, but trust us when we tell you that there truly is only one God for our planet. The name you call Him by doesn't matter one bit. When one religion does not accept the others, we consider it a cult because it misguides people and is preying on the innocent.

You say that it is very calm in heaven, but you can hear everyone and everything here on earth. How is this?

It is difficult to explain, but we have two different planes here which are separated by a weak force field. When we wish to come to you, we just push through it. If we wish to retreat back to the calm silence of Heaven, we return by just pushing back.

When we pray to God or Jesus, should we actually be praying directly to you the earthly spirits?

Yes, you should be praying directly to us as we are the only spirits listening to you. Prayers are not listened to by heavenly spirits or by God, but just by us. We do what we can to help sensible prayers.

Do you prefer that we pray collectively or alone?

We cannot hear you well unless you are on your own as it is very confusing to us when there is more than one person present. However, it is still nice for you to go to church, whether you pray there or not, as it is a very spiritual place.

Does God have any personal influence over when we die, or why we die, on an individual basis?

God and His heavenly spirits are not concerned with us as individuals. This need not worry or concern you. We earth spirits are here to take responsibility for you and, as far as we are able, to look after you from the cradle to the grave. We are also there along with the rest of your previous family from Earth to meet you and to see you through the spiritual tunnel from Earth to Heaven.

What will God do eventually?

He has made what He set out to do – produce us humans and spirits. He is now monitoring the world, His own special planet. One day, should the planet become uninhabitable, He will take us all with him and return to elsewhere in the universe from where He came.

Will God create any new creatures from us?

No. He has finished the work He chose to do on this planet. He has now created His dream and does not want to look further. We are more than He ever hoped for and He is very proud of us.

What are God's feelings about the progress of His spiritual kingdom?

We do not know His feelings, but everything we hear tells us that He is pleased with the progress made on earth.

God has no concern about what we are, what we were on Earth or how we look physically. He is aware of our achievements and very proud of the way that our technology has progressed. This does not include the problems caused through global warming. Our feelings here in the spirit world are that we will continue to develop in the human and spiritual forms, gaining more and more knowledge as the years pass by. Remember it is only when we enter the spiritual world that we actually become God's children.

When God finally decides the time is right or is forced to move on, we will travel with Him and His heavenly spirits across the universe. We feel this knowledge that we have gained on earth now has a purpose and will eventually be used towards the development of other planets. Our knowledge will be utilised and used to speed up the development of other new forms of life. We feel that we now have a very special long-term purpose as we will in effect act on God's behalf as His ambassadors and teachers working alongside His heavenly spirits.

While you have the opportunity, learn as much as you can in your physical form because you will take that knowledge with you.

Chapter 2

THE SPIRIT VERSION OF THE BIBLE AND ITS CHARACTERS

Moses

Who was Moses?

No such person. He's just an invented character in a story.

Samson and Delilah

Samson was a short, healthy, strong and good-looking man, who worked on the land with his father. When Samson was seventeen years old, his father despaired of him because of his gallivanting around with all the local girls. He was considered to be the local Romeo.

Delilah was Samson's first real love. She adored him: they were very close and he told her all his secrets. They wanted children, but could not have them and she miscarried every time she was pregnant. He would not marry her because of this. Eventually, he left Delilah temporarily and married.

Samson married very young, but he continued to have many affairs with the local women because of their attraction to him because of his good looks. His wife never expected Samson to be faithful or any different because she knew exactly what he was when she married him. He did adore his wife, but she was more like a servant to him. She kept his house clean and she cooked for him, but their marriage was more one of convenience than a marriage made of love.

Prior to this when Samson was twenty-three years old, he fell in love with a seventeen-year-old girl. The girl was very beautiful with a perfect figure. He loved her more than she loved him, which was well known in their village. They had a very close relationship for some ten months, but she fell pregnant and when her family found out, they took her away. She gave birth to Samson's son, but it was kept a secret within their families as she was very poor and Samson came from a middle class family.

However, Samson did go and visit his son. The mother of Samson's son eventually married a much older man, with whom she was very happy and she went on to have another child with him. When she gave birth to her second child, Samson was no longer allowed to go and visit his son.

Samson loved his secret son. Being forbidden to see him any more was one of the reasons that caused him to be bitter towards women later on in his life as well as the fact that his mother and other family had forbidden him to be with the woman he loved and wanted to spend his life with.

Samson also brought shame to three other women in their village, but they did not hide away with their illegitimate children as they wanted to be with him.

Eventually, his way of life and not being able to see his secret son caused him to carry lots of anger inside him. This led him to drink, which, in turn, kept on getting him into trouble with the authorities. His health also deteriorated in his later years. Samson suffered from both arthritis and breathing difficulties, but his wife looked after him throughout the period of his illness.

Samson was a hard worker and never asked for anything. He was well known for his feats of strength and this gave him a following amongst the people. However, he was not as strong as everyone made him out to be. He was the type of man who would cheat you for his own gain. Samson's hair was just past his ears in length and it had nothing to do with his strength. That is just a myth. He was noted for being very kind to people and would help anyone, especially if they were poor. He was a legend in his own time and what we would call a Good Samaritan. He had his own beliefs and tried to help everybody, mostly by doing jobs for favours rather than payment.

Samson and his father never saw eye to eye and they disagreed over many things. In particular, Samson did not like the way he treated his mother, as he frequently shouted at her. He threatened his father, but never actually harmed him. Despite this, Samson's father left his land to his son when he died.

The soldiers of the time were afraid of Samson's growing popularity and because of that feared that he might be a subversive. Therefore, they put him into prison, but this was just an excuse. The real reason that they imprisoned Samson was because of his love affair with one of the soldier's wives. It was Delilah that betrayed him as she was jealous of his wife and still loved him. She told the soldiers the secret of the affair with Samson and the soldier's wife, and also encouraged their belief that he was involved in subversive activities.

When they imprisoned Samson, the authorities decided to make an example of him and prove to the people that they were stronger than he was. They did this by cutting off his hair. The guards treated Samson dreadfully, including starvation with just some water to drink for a period of two weeks or more. Finally, the soldiers stabbed him with a sword and then threw him into the lions' den, where he was eaten alive. He never once moaned or shouted while they were killing him. The story of Samson bringing the house down killing three thousand Philistines and himself was not true.

Salome

When Salome met John the Baptist, she fell in love with him, but he did not return her feelings as he did not like either her or her mother. He thought they were both wicked and evil. Later on, as time went by, he had a sexual relationship with Salome's daughter and this caused her to be very jealous, just as it would today. The daughter was very slim and pretty, and John had a weakness for such women.

When Salome found out that John the Baptist was being held captive by the king, Salome persuaded Herod Antepas, the son of King Herod the Great, to have him killed. However, John had already died of his wounds. Therefore, when Salome was told that it was too late for John to be killed, she asked for his head to be brought to her on a platter so that she could spit on it. That was all she was able to do. The rest of the story has been all made up.

Noah

Noah did have an Ark, but it was not because he thought that there were going to be weeks of floods. How could he have known? He was not a magician. The Ark was really for him and his family to emigrate to another country. They merely wanted to take their animals and pets with them for breeding purposes. They built a boat that was about seventy-five feet long and made of local wood. It was built on three levels, but it was not very well designed. Noah's family and friends were very excited about the venture and it was the talk of all the area at that time.

Unfortunately, due to the poor design of the boat and some rough weather, the boat sank soon after it was launched. Not surprisingly, as is the case with a lot of hearsay, the original story was exaggerated into a legend.

King Herod the Great

The first King Herod, who was later called 'King Herod the Great,' was born in 73 BC and was only three years old when Jesus' father, Joseph, was born. They came from different regions that were frequently at war with one another. Herod was an Edomite and of Arabic origin on both sides of his family. Joseph was from the House of David and born into a wealthy and influential Jewish family that was both well connected and owned a substantial amount of land. Joseph was not a carpenter. Neither did he ever live permanently in Nazareth.

Herod and Joseph knew each other as children. They did not like each other either then or later.

Years on, a dispute arose between them because Joseph believed that Herod had tried to cheat him over the ownership of some land. This was not true, but yet another reason for animosity to grow between them.

It was widely known that Herod wished to own and control all the land around Jerusalem. As this would include lands belonging to Joseph and his family, there was an obvious rift and power struggle between them. There was also jealousy.

Many of the people felt that Herod was not the rightful king and that he just held the throne because of his influence with the Roman occupying armies. Judea was a Roman province at the time and there were many people who would have preferred a king from the House of David, perhaps even Joseph himself, rather than Herod. So there was plenty to fuel the jealousy and the power struggle that existed between the two men. Therefore, both would have taken the opportunity to cause harm to the other at any time.

At some stage, there was a conflict between royal troops and soldiers who were more loyal to Joseph. This conflict was also linked to a dispute over the land ownership. In the skirmish, one of Herod's numerous illegitimate sons, a boy of about seventeen years old, who was much loved by his father, was killed by young soldier on the other side. This young soldier was a more experienced fighter from amongst Joseph's supporters.

Herod was enraged and was out for revenge. A rumour reached Herod that Joseph had a love child, a son, by Mary, a serving girl in his father's household. Herod set about making every effort to find the son of Joseph with the intention of a revenge killing. He did this by pretending to hold a census of all infants so that they could eventually be enlisted for service in his army when they were older. This was the reason for the search for Jesus that is described in the Bible.

Joseph's son was named Jesus. He had been placed in the temple as an orphan and under a false name. This had been done to protect him as Joseph suspected that Herod would try and seek his revenge. Herod never found Jesus and eventually gave up the search. The only people who knew the truth about Jesus' parentage were his own teacher and just one other person, Mary Magdalene. No harm came to Jesus at this time in his life and there was never any Slaughter of the Innocents as described in the Bible.

Throughout much of his life, Herod was a sick man. He suffered from stomach problems, which were probably caused by his passion for raw or undercooked red meat. He was in his fifties when he caught a fever and died. Herod believed that his illness and his many sins throughout his lifetime would probably prevent him from going to Heaven when he died. He could do very little about his sins over the years. Nevertheless, he did pray for forgiveness, although deep down he did not believe he would be forgiven.

One thing that he did believe was that without the burden of his diseased body, there just might be a chance of going to Heaven. Therefore, he gave orders that he was not to be buried upon his death, but was to be cremated and his ashes scattered over the sands near to his favourite place, just a few miles from both Jerusalem and Bethlehem.

Saint John the Baptist

John the Baptist was famous for his baptising of the general public, the poor and also criminals who were to be hanged or executed in some other way because of their crimes. He gave these criminals God's blessing before their execution. This was one of the reasons for his popularity and great following with the people, but it also made him unpopular with the rulers.

When John was travelling through Jerusalem baptising people, he saw Jesus coming towards him with his own followers. John was very worried that Jesus would find out that he was really just a charlatan and not a religious person at all, so he decided to approach him.

John baptised Jesus and praised him, telling him that he was stronger and better than him. This was just something he said, but he did not really mean it, as John was frightened that when they met, Jesus and his followers would find out that he was not really the religious man he made himself out to be.

John was making a good living for himself and his family with his activities. He had learnt that by baptising people and gathering crowds of people around to watch, he could both charge for the baptism and also take a collection of money for the Church from the crowd. The money was not going to the Church at all. John's activities up and down the country covered a much larger territory than Jesus, who only preached in and around Jerusalem. After meeting Jesus, John thought that it was safer for him to keep his distance from him, even though they had got on well during the short time they were together.

One morning, very early, John set off to his next baptising venue. He took his friends with him and there were about twenty of them. The Romans had become very worried about John's increasing popularity and they felt that he was the type of person who was likely in secret to form his own army in order to start an uprising against them. Therefore, they set an ambush up for him and attacked him and his friends.

Some of the group were killed and some were injured, including John. The injured were taken prisoner and the Roman soldiers took every one of them, including the dead, back with them. This was to ensure that they did not leave any evidence behind them so that there would be no backlash from the people over the killings of religious people.

John died on the way to prison from the sword wound that had punctured his heart. All of John's group were placed in cells and eventually died from either their wounds or starvation.

Mary Magdalene

Mary was a very wealthy and educated woman, who also had political influence and aspirations, which was very unusual for a woman in those days. Her mother died fairly young and her father died not much later at the age of thirty-seven years.

Because of her wealth and generosity, some of the more extreme religious groups welcomed her in. She was a friend of Jesus' mother, Mary. When delivering food and flowers to the temple, she would also check that he was well looked after and happy so that she could report back on his progress.

Mary Magdalene had a brother who was also named Joseph, who died in battle at the age of twenty-two years from a sword wound to his chest. Joseph was a popular figure in the area and therefore he had a big funeral. The place where he was buried, on his family's land, has now been covered over.

Later in life, Mary had a problem with brittle bones and particularly in her legs. Mary died at the age of thirty-nine years when Jesus was about eleven years old. There is no truth in the story that she married Jesus and had children by him. Similarly, there is no truth in the claims from the Bible that Mary Magdalene was present either at the death of Jesus or was involved in events after his death because she died before Jesus even came of age.

Joseph

Joseph, the father of Jesus, came from a wealthy family of landowners and traders who employed many people. He was not a carpenter and he did not live in Nazareth as the Bible says.

Joseph and his family were all Jews from the House of David, and he was a tall man for his time. Joseph's family had a large property inside the wall of Jerusalem, next to one of the entrances of the city. He also owned a lot of land nearby, which was mainly agricultural, but he kept his animals there.

Mary, the mother of Jesus, worked for Joseph and when they started to have a relationship, it was kept secret because he already had three wives. Mary, who was a stunningly beautiful girl, became pregnant and gave birth to Jesus, her second child with Joseph. Jesus was born in a room in the servants' quarters of his father's house in Jerusalem. Jesus was not born in Bethlehem nor was he ever in a manger.

Joseph wished the relationship, and his children that were born to Mary, to remain a secret. This was because Mary was just a servant and it was frowned upon for a man in his position to have such an association. Therefore, Joseph and Mary agreed to send Jesus to a temple inside the wall of Jerusalem and near to where he was born to be brought up by the priests. Jesus was taken to the temple within one hour of his birth. Joseph never disowned his son and always provided for him, but this was in secret.

Judas Iscariot

Judas was born the son of Jacob who, in turn, came from a long line of soldiers in the Roman army. Judas joined the Roman army at the age of fourteen years. He was not really strong enough to be a soldier, but his father pushed him into it. Jacob also ensured that he had a good, safe position in the army. Judas was not a nasty man. He was a kind and happy man. Although a Roman citizen, he respected other people and different nationalities, and would help people whenever he could.

At the time of Jesus' demise, Judas had risen to the position of commander of his own force, a unit in the Roman army. He rode around with a horse and chariot. Judas had a family that included three brothers. He never married and did not have any children.

When Judas found out about the arrest of Jesus, he went to the jail and into the cell where Jesus and the other prisoners were held. His position allowed him to move freely in and out of the jail, but he was not allowed by his superiors to take any food in to feed the prisoners. He did sympathise with Jesus, but was unable to help him for fear of angering his superiors, who would have simply killed him as well.

Judas was in the cell after Jesus died. When the last of the two robbers were taken out to be executed, they left two pieces of silver shaped like large engraved coins. Judas simply picked them up and took them: nothing more. This is the only true part of the pieces of silver legend. Judas did not commit suicide. He was thirty-six years old when Jesus died and continued to live to the age of fifty-four years, although for the last six years of his life, he was very ill. He was buried in the local cemetery in Bethlehem and if you can find the records there, it will be documented.

The Virgin Mary

Mary worked as a servant to Joseph's family for eleven years. Joseph was a wealthy man and Mary had a secret relationship with him that lasted for several years. The reason for the secrecy over the relationship was because he was already married with three wives.

In those days, as she was a lowly servant girl, it was frowned upon for him to go below his station and have a relationship with her. However, she was extremely beautiful. She was small, only just five feet tall, with long, black hair and he was deeply infatuated with her beauty. Although just a servant, Mary was treated like a princess in the servants' quarters and ate separately from the others and much better food.

At the age of eighteen, Mary had a daughter by Joseph, but she was given to a member of her family to be brought up due to the fact that she was the result of a relationship with her master. Unfortunately, she died at the age of three years due to stomach problems. Later, Mary gave birth to Jesus, and he, too, had to be fostered because of Joseph being the father and his status in the community. Jesus was secretly handed over to the temple, as at that time, King Herod was seeking revenge for the death of his son by Joseph. Mary's relationship with Joseph later ended and she fell in love with and married someone else.

Seven years later, she gave birth to another son named Jonathan. He was also sent away and lived until he was twenty-five years of age. Mary suffered from heart disease and circulation problems that affected her right leg. Due to her ill-health, Mary did not live a long life, but died after being terribly ill for quite a long time. At the request of Joseph, Mary's body was buried in his garden inside the wall of Jerusalem near to where their son, Jesus, is now buried.

Jesus Christ

Jesus was born in Jerusalem and not in Bethlehem as the Bible states. Mary, his mother, was only allowed to cuddle him briefly before he was taken away from her. Within an hour, as pre-arranged, he was taken secretly to the temple grounds, which were nearby.

Joseph paid for his upbringing in the temple. This was kept as a secret and Jesus grew up thinking he was just another sponsored orphan. He was one of over a dozen children in the temple schools at that time. They were mostly all in a similar position, sent from wealthy families and paid for to be educated by the temple. Some knew their parents; some did not. The temple fostered and educated these children as it was then the only way they could receive a regular income aside from charity.

Once there, Jesus was received by a gentle, devout and very spiritual old priest, Jacob, who had been assigned to take care of him. Part of his duties was to feed and clothe the boy and he was also to be his personal tutor. Jacob was the only personal tutor Jesus had throughout his lifetime. Jacob and the temple itself were well paid by Joseph, in secret, for caring for the boy, bringing Him up and attending to His general well-being.

Jesus grew up with Jacob caring for him day-to-day and he settled down after a few months to become a quiet and contented baby. He had a regular routine, which babies love. He was fed at regular times and with good food and clean water. He was washed regularly and had no difficulty sleeping in the quiet surroundings of the huge temple complex of buildings.

As he grew up, Jesus was a very tidy and clean boy, and never wasted water. He had a teacher whom he loved very much and came to regard him as a father figure. The teacher taught him to read and write. It was this man who told him that he had the gift of healing. Jacob also taught Jesus how to use his left hand for guidance to the painful areas and to use his right hand to heal. He also taught him to pray to God and the spirits.

Jesus grew to be a healthy young lad. He was very mischievous, always trying to get into cupboards and drawers. He loved to hide away in places where he hoped Jacob would have a job to find him. This may well have been an inclination that helped him years later when he was frequently hiding or on the run from Roman soldiers and the men of the local religious leaders of the Sanhedrin.

Jesus was fond of his food and had a particular preference for fruit and particularly oranges. The people who looked after Jesus had to be careful as, if not watched, he would eat the skins as well. In those days, no one ever thought to wash fruit before eating it as water was a very valuable commodity.

As a little crawling infant, Jesus would save fruit seeds to play with and loved the noise that they made when shaken, rather like babies love the sound of a rattle. Jesus also loved to be able to put his feet into warm water whenever he was allowed to due to the scarcity of water and seemed to get a lot of comfort from this.

At around the age of four years, the priests noticed that Jesus liked to screw up cloth into a ball. If he could, he would tie it up tight in a ball shape and kick it about on the floor. He also liked hiding in cupboards, behind doors and dark places for Jacob and others to find him. Jesus also particularly liked to stand at the slatted window of his living quarters and watch the people go about their business in the street below. Jesus wanted very much to go outside, but was not allowed to.

However, he quickly learned that it was not safe for any little boys to be out alone. Unknown to him, this was especially so for him as his father had enemies everywhere. So Jesus would spend many hours standing, watching and listening at the 'window' and would often cry if he were taken away from it for his lessons.

Jesus learned to read and write very early and was a bright pupil. He would work very hard for a couple of hours, but then he would lose interest and want to get back to his vantage point at the window. In general, he was a good child and it was never necessary to shout at him or smack him. Jacob or one of the other priests would only need to raise a finger and wag it at Jesus and he would do as he was told. Despite being an obedient child, Jesus had a considerable sense of mischief. He would hide people's shoes when they were not watching. In so many ways, he was just like any other child.

He lived in the temple precincts with about ten other boys. Mostly they were older than him. They, too, were brought up by other teachers and therefore had different ways to Jesus. There was one boy who was a very slow learner and Jesus always tried to read to him and help him with his lessons. He had also been put into the temple by his father, who was a very wealthy man like Jesus' own father. Money was no object for this boy's family, but they did not want him at home because it was shameful for people to have what we would consider to be a backward or a retarded child.

Jesus taught him to do simple things like washing and dressing himself, cleaning floors and so on, and they became great friends. Jesus helped the boy, whose name was John, throughout his childhood and later years as well. John even died within a short time of Jesus. It was thought that the boy died because of his grief over the loss of his greatest friend and the manner of that friend's death.

By the time Jesus was nine years old, his tutor, Jacob, was teaching him about spiritual things and also about simple and natural healing. He taught

Jesus what the temple expected of him in return for his care and education. This was to encourage Jesus to earn a living for himself and to help other children that were in the care of the temple. One of Jesus' greatest desires had always been to go out of the confines of the temple and to meet people and to help them as he had been taught.

Jesus was not at all afraid of strangers as he had so often watched them passing by from his window and had listened to them. He used to see people meeting together and chatting, and he realised that this was how people learned from each other about travellers and events that were happening at that time as there was no other method of communication than the spoken word. Most people could not read at that time in history, so they could not even use the few manuscripts and scrolls that did exist.

His teacher died when Jesus was about ten or eleven years old. Jesus was heartbroken. It was then that he started to venture outside. He believed that if he healed people, this would somehow help bring Jacob back to him. He became a storyteller, telling people all the stories that Jacob had taught him.

A short time later, he also preached outside the walls of Jerusalem, but always had to hide away from the Romans. He was careful enough to make sure that he was always surrounded by people, so it would be easier to hide from them. He always dressed in a similar fashion to the people in the streets so that he could mingle with the crowd easily if there was danger around. This particularly appealed to Jesus as he had always enjoyed hiding as a young child.

People were fascinated by the young Jesus and his story-telling abilities. They not only listened to him, but sought him out on other occasions as they wanted to hear more. Slowly, he gathered more and more small groups of people and a following that later became crowds.

It was about then that he started touching people in order to heal them. He usually touched their heads as he prayed for them as Jacob had taught him or as they spoke to him. His hands were soft, just like a woman's, and he would lay them on wherever the person had pain. He quickly learned how strong his healing powers were and that they were growing stronger and stronger. Very quickly, the word spread about Jesus' remarkable gift of healing and more and more people were coming to the temple for help. They would beg Jesus to lay his hands on them so that they could receive healing from him.

In return for his help, they would bring him small gifts of food, fruit and money. Jesus never personally accepted any of the gifts that were brought to him. They were always given to the temple. To the young Jesus, it was his dream coming true after so many years of looking at people on the street below from inside the temple.

At the age of twelve years, because of the fear and threats to his life, he stopped preaching outside. He carried on preaching and healing secretly inside the temple and its grounds. People that needed healing would quietly go into the temple precincts during the daytime.

Eventually, he was holding healing sessions several times a day. It made him very happy, but also very tired, so that he would have to go back to his room and sleep deeply, sometimes for several hours. Jesus often felt very lonely in his single room and asked if his friend John could share the room with him. This was allowed and really helped Jesus to relax and gain in confidence.

His friend John still had many problems, and even with speaking. Jesus was the only one person who always seemed to be able to understand what John was trying to say and he was very patient and kind to him at all times. They loved each other like brothers.

Jesus would always pray at night. He would kneel and speak to God and ask Him to make everyone better. He did not know any other way to pray and at that young age, he did not know or understand who or where God was. Jesus prayed because he had been taught by Jacob that it was the right thing to do.

As Jesus reached his early teens, there were so many people coming to see him that the Romans and others began to get suspicious as to what was really happening. There were many occasions when they actually stopped people and questioned and searched them before they entered the temple. Because of this, Jesus decided that it was time to gather his courage and to go out healing and preaching in public again in order to divert the unwanted attention away from the temple.

Jesus started venturing outside of the temple into the streets and wandering into the crowds that were everywhere. Wherever he went, he would gather people around him with his stories and then lay hands on them to help heal them. It was common for him to go out once or twice in a day and often to stay out until it grew dark. This was because he enjoyed what he was doing so much. He would never stay out in the dark as he did not feel safe, but during his trips outside of the temple, he would gather people around and preach and heal them.

By this time, many of the people were beginning

to realise there was someone very special amongst them. They all wanted to listen to Jesus and have him lay his hands upon them. Even the people themselves realised that the large crowds would draw the attention of the occupying Roman troops so they kept the groups as small as possible in order not draw attention to Jesus and his activities.

The people did not want any harm to come to Jesus and they made every effort to keep things quiet and to keep him hidden. If any soldiers or suspicious people came near, Jesus would simply hide in the crowd. He looked and dressed like everyone else and, as the crowd dispersed, he would slip away back to the temple grounds.

The Romans had heard over the previous few years that there was a young man preaching and healing. Consequently, they set about to try and catch him, but never managed to do so as there were always people around him. They now realised that the young man that the people were calling 'Rabbi' was the child that they had previously been looking for.

Jesus enjoyed his work preaching and healing, but when, as sometimes happened, he was unable to cure an individual, he would become very distressed and upset. He would call upon the spirits as Jacob had taught him and ask them why they could not – or would not – help him. Jesus was always questioning himself and his abilities, and especially his failures.

Even when he was a young adolescent, he was never interested in girls or women. He had his close friend John and believed that this friend would always be there for him and that he, Jesus, would always be there for him too. This friendship gave him all the companionship he needed. His friend would also copy Jesus and try to heal people, but he did not have the gift. Jesus would sometimes get some of his other followers to pretend they were ill so that John could try to heal them. This made his friend John very happy.

Jesus and John were very, very close growing up in the temple together and they were often likened to twins. The spirits have told me that it was some of them who had sent this boy, John, to be Jesus' companion, so he could learn deep friendship and compassion, and how to love and care for people.

Jesus always had time to listen to his teachers and others and to learn from them. It was the temple teacher, Jacob, who gave him his original belief in God and helped Jesus to understand that other people had their own different beliefs which must be respected, but that it was his role to show them the true path of the spirit world.

Jesus had a very soft, gentle but penetrating voice. He seldom raised his voice or got angry with others. Even when he did things like turn over the money tables in the temple and shout at the cheats and liars, it was only for show. He did not really lose his temper. People would gather anywhere they heard Jesus was just to hear his voice.

Jesus was described as being like a bright star. Although he was quiet and unassuming in his ways, he had the ability to light up the whole of the city. He had total control over the crowds that gathered around him. Also he had the ability both to get and to hold their attention as he preached, told his stories and healed the sick.

The authorities were not bothered about the stories Jesus told, but they were very suspicious of the large crowds and massive following that he was drawing from afar and also because of his healing abilities.

Over time, Jesus began to grow frustrated at the limitations and restrictions that were placed on his preaching and healing due to the presence of the Roman soldiers. He began to venture further from the city walls and would often go down near to the river to preach. This meant that very often a large group of people would soon gather around him. There were other preachers there, but he always drew large crowds with his healing abilities. Jesus became stronger and stronger as a healer, and the word spread everywhere of his extraordinary healing powers.

The large crowds that Jesus attracted were getting bigger and bigger, and they would clamour and push one other just to see him or to touch his clothing. Jesus tried to vary the place, time and day of his teaching sessions for security reasons, but the news would always leak out and he would arrive to find masses of would-be listeners. Everyone knew him, but outside of his own immediate group of followers, he did not really know anyone. To Jesus they were just the faces of people in need of help.

From time to time, Jesus would see a woman looking at him. He eventually found out that her name was Mary, but he did not know that she was his own mother and he treated her no differently than any other. Jesus was enjoying his life in spite of the danger in which he was constantly placing himself. Preaching and healing was what he had always wanted to do from a very young age and it was Jacob that had instilled this passion in him and made him believe in himself. By this time, the Romans and other leaders were sure that the young man was Jesus who was the child from the temple. They had grown to fear his popularity as they thought he might try to use it to raise an army from amongst the Jews.

Eventually, there came the time when Jesus had agreed to speak with a particular group of men who were all criminals and they asked him to forgive them and to heal them. Jesus agreed, although his friends warned him not to go. The weather was misty with rain and visibility was poor, which meant that Roman soldiers and spies were able to mingle in with the crowd and remain undetected. Jesus met the criminals and started to speak to them. He then realised that the Romans were hidden all around him in the crowd.

Despite this, Jesus thought he could help the criminals and then disappear quickly into the crowd and avoid arrest by the Romans. Unfortunately, that was not to be. In no time, the hidden Romans alerted the soldiers and the whole group was rounded up and arrested. Jesus and eight others, including some of the criminals and some of his temple followers, were arrested and imprisoned.

The Romans then starved the group for some days, which was a classic Roman method of treating prisoners in order to lower their resistance. For two days, he and his friends were starved of food, but given water. The reality is that there was no such event as a Last Supper for Jesus, no breaking of bread and no drinking of wine from the Holy Grail. Jesus went to his death hungry.

On the third day of the group's imprisonment, the Romans strapped each of the prisoners to crudely-made crosses and they were marched up to the top of a small hill in a procession. No-one was nailed to their cross. Metal nails were not used as they were too costly. They were just tied to it with their arms apart to keep them from protecting themselves or kicking out against what was to come. Jesus did not at any time wear a crown of thorns. Nobody proclaimed him to be King of the Jews, but along with all the others, he was beaten and whipped.

Up on the hill, the Romans tied their prisoners' feet to the bases of the crosses and laid all the captives on the ground with blankets underneath them in order to soak up the blood which was to be shed. They were all placed in a circle with their feet towards the middle. Then came perhaps the most touching moment of the entire story.

Mary, Jesus' mother, was there in the crowd. Weeping and sobbing, she managed to push her way through the crowd and, when she thought no-one was watching, she went up to Jesus. Mary stood there looking down at her son with pity and great sorrow. With a sad expression on his face, he looked up at her and said: 'I know you, Mary. I have seen you many times in among the crowds of people that I have taught and also in the temple courtyard. Tell me, Mary, who are you?'

Mary bent down and placed her hands on his head as if to smooth his hair and wipe the sweat and tears from his face. Quietly so that no-one would hear her, she told Jesus the long-hidden truth. 'I am your mother, Jesus,' she said. 'I am your real mother and I love you as I always have done over the years that I watched you grow up without you ever knowing it. I love you and will do so for all of my life. I shall look after your body and care for it.'

At that point, some of the guards noticed her. They came over and pulled her away. Jesus and Mary were not able to speak to each any more, but his eyes were full of tears as he watched her go back to her place with the other women in the noisy crowd. Time after time from that moment until the very end, his eyes searched constantly for his mother in the crowd and fixed on her whenever he spotted her again.

Although he was the gentlest individual in the group, Jesus was still the bravest and the only one to shout at the soldiers 'I am not a thief. I am not a rogue. You have taken the wrong man.' Unfortunately, this was to no avail. All of their wrists were slashed open and the crowds stoned them on the orders of the Roman soldiers as they lay there bleeding and dying in the sun. Jesus, resigned to his fate, spoke for the last time – 'Forgive them, my God. Forgive them. Please forgive those who kill me and my friends.'

All the priests from the temple and Jesus' followers watched what happened and feared for their own lives. When all of the group were dead, the soldiers untied them, wrapped cloth around their bodies, secured the cloth with cord and put them all into a cart to carry them to a cave. Jesus and the others were placed in a cave by the Romans and it was blocked with a small boulder.

They did this to prevent Jesus' followers from plundering his grave for souvenirs and fragments of his clothing or body that might have healing powers for them. In fact, had the followers but known it – and for the same reasons, – the Romans had chopped off both of Jesus' hands before dumping him in the cave. They felt that if he were ever to come back to life, the absence of his healing hands would mean he would be less of a threat.

That same night, under the cover of darkness and acting on instructions from Jesus' mother, Joseph of

Arimathea, a friend of the family, along with five of his loyal servants, came and secretly took the body of Jesus away. They took his body down the hill, through an arched door in the wall of the city of Jerusalem and took him to his father's own family garden to be buried. This location was known only to Joseph of Arimathea, Mary, a few close friends and the servants who were working under Joseph of Arimathea's orders.

To this day, Jesus' grave remains completely untouched with the cloth that he was wrapped in and his bodily remains intact. When found, it can be easily identified, as the place where he lies is carved out of the stone and it has a stone 'lid' with another stone on top. This was done as they thought it was extra protection to prevent his body being stolen or his grave plundered. Mary, his mother, is also buried nearby in the grounds of the property, but in a normal grave.

Three days after his death, Jesus was believed to have been sighted outside of the cave where he had been placed by the Romans, but this was only his spirit which had come to ensure that the others who were buried there were able to pass peacefully over into Heaven.

This phenomenon caused many people to flock to the cave because it was the first time an important person had returned from the dead. The excitement of the crowd outside the cave for the next two days led to the Roman soldiers pulling the boulder back to show the crowd that he was truly dead. However, they found instead that he was not there. His body had disappeared. The crowd naturally thought that he had risen from the dead because of the sightings of his spirit a few days before.

After this tragic event, the followers of Jesus feared for their own lives and fled the area. Over the next six months, many of them were rounded up by the Romans and killed in the same way as Jesus. Their bodies were taken down the hill from where Jesus had died and they were just thrown in a ditch. The local people were then forced to fill in the ditch or risk losing their own lives.

The people who knew the whereabouts of Jesus' resting place visited his grave in secret. Servants and even soldiers loyal to Joseph of Arimathea went and prayed there. Flowers were put on the grave, but only at night, so that the Romans could not see them. Only the chosen few were allowed to be buried inside the walls of Jerusalem.

Even as he was being put to death, few spoke out against his unfair treatment or raised their voices on his behalf. The people were very afraid of the Roman authorities and what they would do to them in turn. Nobody cried out that Jesus was a holy man and should be spared. Only a small group of women tried to speak up, but women counted for very little in their society and the soldiers quickly and roughly escorted them away.

Jesus was a devout Jew. He did not proclaim himself to be the Son of God. He did not know who his mother and father were, and he never heard of a virgin birth in his lifetime. Jesus never put himself forward as anything but a dedicated holy man and healer. He is now here in the spirit world and rests here exactly like all the others of us.

Chapter 3

A DIRECT MESSAGE FROM JESUS CHRIST

Lilian James told us [the authors] she had received a message from Jesus saying that he wants all the truths about him to be told at last. He wants us to know that he was just a man much like everyone else and that he was treated very badly by the Roman soldiers.

He feels that stories about his life have been blown up out of all proportion. People were then afraid of what they wanted to believe in. He says that the Bible is a mix of many stories with many things that were quoted actually being impossible to happen to mankind, with many people reading them but not really believing them.

'How can somebody be turned to stone? They cannot,' Jesus said. 'How could I turn water into wine? I could not. I was no different from anyone else. I could feel that I had healing powers and was guided by my holy spirit to preach. This I did just around the walls of Jerusalem away from the Roman soldiers. I did not let them see me. I still pray, but now I do not need to hide anymore.'

Jesus still prays in his white cloak and he said he has no objection to us locating his resting place and opening the grave. He does wish his body to be found, but not yet a while.

I [Lilian] asked whether he liked and approved of the fuss and stories now told about him. He said that in general he did, though he did not care for the lies that were told and deplored the way some people who believed the exaggerated stories have fought and killed each other and strangers because of the nonsense. He said, further, that he regards the Bible as a gift, as his crown. He now rests in the spirit world with his former human earthly, but now spirit, mother and father, and their many descendants still mostly in the region of Jerusalem.

Chapter 4

THE SPIRIT WORLD

Please will you describe the spirit world for us?

It's wonderful. Absolutely wonderful. You could hardly believe how wonderful it is. I suppose I see pretty much the same as you see, but it's somehow much more beautiful. It is hard for you to imagine how it is. If you imagine that you are looking into space at night with the stars twinkling and how peaceful that makes you feel, that is what it is like here in Heaven. That is what I see. I can see the stars, too… and beyond them more and more beautiful stars and lights. Lots of colours out there.

There is also another planet far out only just visible. That planet has its own spirit world, but we can't talk to them yet. And they don't talk to us. They say we will be able to talk later. The floor of this spirit world is like cloud… sort of fleecy and the air is very pure. It looks just as if you are looking at the stars all twinkling and shining everywhere. It is very quiet here. There's no sound at all, just very peaceful quiet. Silence. Even when another spirit passes by me, it is still silent. Completely soundless.

There are lots of other planets and stars out in the universe, but we can never go to the far end of it because there is no far end. It just goes on and on forever. We don't know where the sun came from. I hear that it and everything else was once part of another much bigger more huge mass of stuff and our sun and other suns broke away and went into space. I don't understand these things so I don't try.

We know from the heavenly spirits that it is possible for them to travel much further and it is even more incredibly beautiful further away. But everything here on our planet came from the sun. It is a living thing… just a living fragment of one of those other even bigger suns.

We ourselves have two forms. One is like a shadow, but it resembles the shape and colour we had before we became spirits. The other is a globe shape like God Himself has, only a lot smaller. That's what shape we take when we want to travel. Travel is very exciting to us. When I ask for my family or others I know to be near me, the message goes out directly from me without a sound and they come. We pass messages to each other also silently.

Things are very happy here. We are all happy. The only time we get disturbed is when we try to put something right for you, but there is opposition from other spirits… perhaps someone else's family who is involved and they are trying to help someone else. That can cause friction and difficulties.

We can't stop another spirit doing what they think is right. We can only influence things for you and hope we succeed. For example, if someone was going to kill someone else, we could not stop them. Not even if there is a good reason to stop them and get them sent to prison or something. I think that's a pity, but that's the way it is.

Eventually, though, we will all have to go. This

planet will fall away and explode, like a huge volcano, I suppose. Anyway, it will get burned up by the sun. At that time, we'll all go into space with God and we all know we will enjoy it. At the moment, we are all spirits who once were ordinary people and we are going to remain here until God takes us to a new planet when the time is right. He knows when and He knows the way. The Earth has already dropped a little further away from the sun and it has slowed down a bit. This is one of the things that is affecting the weather.

We all have families here. It was amazing to me to meet people who had been part of my family long before I was born. Sort of ancestors, really. There is also a special place where spirits can go to rest and get their energy back. This is needed especially for some new spirits when they first get here from the earth. Some had died tragic or sudden or painful deaths. Some have lost energy through long illnesses. They are very weak and bewildered when they get here. We take them to the place where they can rest for a while.

Heaven, you say, is supposedly quiet and peaceful, but you manage to be able to hear and see everything that is happening here on Earth. How is this possible?

In our shadow form we can hear and communicate, but when we revert to our spiritual form, all the noise ceases. We do, however, have to revert to the shadow form to get our energy levels replenished. The two heavens are separated by a force field. One is silent and the other is where we can hear the noise of the earth. Using our energy, we can just push or ease through the force field that separates the two.

55

There are many sightings of ghosts around the world. Are these ghosts different from you and if so, why?

For many possible personal and earthly reasons, these are spirits who have unfinished problems or matters that they feel they cannot yet leave. Usually, these are things that, although they do not realise it, are never going to be solved. The spirits then tend to stay in the same place where things are familiar to them and they feel safe. They really need a good psychic helper or guide to enable them to progress on their way. They are not forced to go to Heaven, but are allowed whatever time it takes until they feel ready.

Until then, they do not pass through the tunnel and they remain where they choose as a cold spirit. This is why when you enter a room where a ghost is present, the room can feel very cool. It is because they have not yet properly passed into the spirit world. Mostly, though, they seem happy in their chosen confinement. However, the majority will accept the help of a psychic or a man or woman of the cloth to send them on their journey to Heaven.

God must be a huge form of spiritual or cosmic energy. Are you able to see Him when you are in Heaven?

Oh yes. We can see Him moving around the earth, but He is much further up than us. His energy form is the shape of a giant globe that glows. From down here, He looks the size of a skyscraper. God is about half as big as the size of the moon. When new spirits come into Heaven and see the globe, they are amazed and often a bit frightened. We have to explain to them who and what He is and that they are perfectly safe.

What is the difference between earthly spirits like you and God's heavenly spirits?

They are heavenly spirits and, unlike us, earthly spirits who were not born through the animal kingdom as we were. They have never experienced that which we possess through having had human life. They do not understand about languages, being able to read, write, paint, mathematics, libraries and so on. They do not have any of the knowledge that an earth-born spirit experiences and possesses. Nor do they possess all the different emotions and memories that we have collected throughout our lifetimes.

Heavenly spirits can travel much faster than we can and can achieve much more. They spend their time controlling the weather and balancing the planet and have their own network of energy tunnels above the ceiling. Our energy tunnels are near the earth's surface. Our job is to look after you.

Have earthly spirits the capability of being able to travel to other planets?

No, we cannot. Spirits from other planets cannot visit us and we cannot leave the earth. We are confined to it due to the atmosphere.

You have mentioned that the spirits stay amongst us on our level. However, are they able to go up higher should they wish to?

We would go to a higher region when all our directly connected family have joined us. This could be three or four generations or more later. Our great-grandchildren would take over from us if we decide to move up as a family unit. They would look after their children and other family, and we would join our forefathers. It is more peaceful above and there is more space.

Does there happen to be a limit to how high you can go in the atmosphere?

We are only permitted to go up as far as God's heavenly spirits allow us to. God has made a kind of field of resistance around the earth, which is in the shape of a sphere. It starts at the tip of the highest mountains in the world. This is for our protection as, at present, we cannot exist in space. Obviously, we can travel higher if we are in an aeroplane travelling with you.

When you go higher up in the atmosphere to wherever you are allowed, apart from it being quieter, does anything else change?

Our movement slows down the further we go up into the atmosphere. However, here below we can move around in the energy tunnels that God has made for us. This enables us to travel very fast over long distances.

If I were to ask you as a spirit a question that you felt would misguide us, are you obliged to answer me?

No. As a spirit, I can refuse to answer and keep secrets if I think that is in your or the family's best interests.

How do spirits interpret the stories and teachings of the Bible?

When we pass over and arrive in Heaven, everything is so different from our beliefs that date back to our childhood. Everything becomes more clear. The Bible contains many basic, commonsense truths, but there are also many parts of the Bible that are just folklore stories.

What is the spiritual theory of how the universe started?

We know for a fact that it was one vast empty space with one gigantic sun. It was alive and burned up all the energy. We also know that it broke up into smaller pieces, with most of them being larger than our planet. So our planet was one of the smallest and it dropped away from the mother sun because it was lighter than the other suns and could not remain in orbit, and started to fall away millions of years ago.

It came with God as we know Him, and the planet travelled for millions of years. All planets have gods and they seem to be guided in their own way. These gods do not usually move around in space a great deal; they prefer to just travel around their own designated planet.

There are more planets and stars out in space than anyone can imagine. It is absolutely enormous and it has no limits... no beginning and no ending. As human beings, we are very lucky as our God has given us two lives. However, the underlying sadness is that in the first life we have to suffer to get to the second one. However, that is the way that it has to be.

Are there any spirits that have haloes?

No.

You say that you possess energy and that you have access at all times to replenish it. Can you also share it or pass it on to other spirits?

We can, but this is not very often necessary. However, if you come into the spirit world and you are weak or sick, we can share our energy with you. This is the same method as when Wilf is using spiritual energy to heal people. It is exactly the same kind of power that Jesus received from the spirit world and then passed on to people. What was really remarkable about Jesus was that he had so very much greater healing powers than others at that particular time in our history.

You say that you are able to read magazines and newspapers, etc. Are you able to do this in the dark?

No, this is not possible. We need light.

Does your IQ stay the same in the spirit world?

Yes. You stay exactly as you are.

As a spirit, can you understand what we are doing when we are reading or writing?

I can take everything directly from your mind through your spirit. We spirits are in contact with our loved ones even when you are not aware of it.

Will there ever be a time when we can all communicate with the spirit world to bring us closer together?

This will never happen, but I hope that people will read this book we are making and have a better understanding of what there is beyond death. There are many, many spirits giving the same message to their loved ones every day through mediums and Spiritualists. Therefore, this book is an opportunity for people to be enlightened. We also want the divisions and wars caused by different religions and beliefs to end.

We know that there is only one God for this planet and that if we all respected Him, each in our own preferred ways, all the religious wars would end. Religious wars account for most of the discord seen worldwide. If all the religious wars ceased, the world would be a much happier place for everyone.

Here in the spirit world, we realise that there is only one God and we all respect Him and are grateful to Him for what He has done for mankind.

Would you please explain the experience you went through as your body died and your spirit passed through to the place we call Heaven?

I was in a coma, but I kept waking up and going back to sleep again. My previous life kept coming back to me and I saw visions of the past from my youth, including my parents and other family.

It felt like I was floating on water, then I closed my eyes and did not wake up again. I was then looking down at my body and the nurse came to my bedside, covered my body over with a sheet and wheeled it away. They took all my medication away, put my clothes into a bundle and waited for somebody to pick them up.

When I went through the tunnel, my baby daughter, Sandra, my first-born, was waiting for me. I was very surprised to see her, but very happy. She then took me to the resting-place to recuperate after my illness. After I had rested, I was told to come to you to try and open up the connection between the physical and spiritual world via Wilf and start the message about the writing of this book.

Were we born before?

Yes, Laurie. You were first born around nine hundred years ago. You were a nineteen-year-old soldier dressed in a white uniform. You were with four other soldiers and were camped at an oasis in the desert. You were captured by the enemy and all five of you were hanged.

Was this the first time that you lived on the earth in the physical form or can you recall having previous lives?

Yes. I was born before. I died aged twenty-four giving birth to my second child, a son.

If we have a second life, what do we remember of the first?

Some children have memories of their previous life. However, the memories generally fade as the child gets older. Strong memories can survive in some people. For example, in instances of violent death and pain, they may remember how they died. You were hanged in your previous life and that is why you dislike fastening the top button of your shirt collar.

Others, who have drowned, may come back with a strong fear of water. These remote memories may be the deep-rooted cause of strong fears that some people have, such as a fear of heights, flying or snakes. There is often a connection that can be discovered.

When we pass on to the spirit world, what happens to our emotions?

When you come to Heaven, you bring all your emotions with you. It is not possible to fall in love as a spirit, but this is not as bad as it sounds. If you were in love with someone while on earth, this love comes with you. Your parents and grandparents came to Heaven with their love and because that included their undying love for you, they will continue to love you and look after you until you, in turn, come to join them.

Are there any other ways in which we can make contact with the spirit world apart from using a clairvoyant or medium?

Yes, there is a method, but there are only 'Yes' or 'No' answers available to questions that you may ask us, plus it's not always very reliable. To do it, you take a small chain, about six inches long. Dangle it from the finger and thumb of your right hand and perpendicularly over the palm of your left hand. Now, keeping both hands completely still, ask your question.

Allow some time for an answer, as the spirit only has its spiritual energy to use to move the chain. Also bear in mind that the spirit may not actually be present at that moment, though that is not usual.

Also the spirit may not know the answer. In both situations, either nothing will happen or the chain may move in a circle.

If the answer is 'Yes,' the chain will swing back and forth towards you, and if the answer is 'No,' it will swing from left to right. If the chain swings clockwise or anti-clockwise (in a circle), this means that the spirit does not understand the question.

Apart from this way of communicating, please always remember that you can pray to us if you need help. It is always worth trying to communicate with us, whatever your reasons for doing so. We are your close and loving friends and family. We are here to care, support and try to help you whenever we can.

Why has there never been this kind of contact before?

No-one has ever asked the questions in the way that you have asked them. I was chosen to initiate the contact with you. I do not know exactly why I was the chosen one, but the basic reason for this was that while people on earth have been fussing about wars and religions and conquering outer space, they have all neglected the inner space and the things that really matter about the planet.

Now things have got so bad, there was no more time to lose. Someone had to get things going quickly. We hope that this book will attract everyone's attention for the good of our planet. The spirit world hopes that this book will benefit everyone on earth and that together we can help to save the planet from further damage and danger, for both us spirits and you humans. After all, you must never forget that the earth is still our planet, too, with us and all our loved ones on it. We are very concerned and very determined to do everything we can to protect it.

Can we humans touch spirits?

No, but we spirits can touch you. We do this when we are trying to heal you or to let you know someone is present. However, although you cannot touch us, you, as humans, can send your thoughts out to us. We hear your prayers and your voices clearly, which is what happens when you pray. We listen and hear, and then do what we think is best for you.

When a person passes over and reaches Heaven, it is a great comfort for them to realise that they can still both communicate with their loved ones even though they are in the spirit world and that they can also hear voices from the human world which they have left behind. You should always remember and be comforted by the knowledge that we are around you, listening, trying to help you and sending you our love always. There's always someone there caring for you and watching over you.

Can we be refused entry into Heaven?

Yes you can, but this refusal can only be made by your own spiritual family. They are the only ones that have this discretionary power. If you have committed a wrongdoing, it is for them – and them alone – to decide whether to forgive you or not. It depends on how much shame you have brought upon them and how much genuine remorse and regret you feel. They make the ultimate decision as to whether to let you come through the tunnel into Heaven or leave you as a ghost at least for a while.

Is there a day-to-day connection between the earthbound spirits like yourselves and the heavenly cosmic spirits above?

They are there to solve problems that we are sometimes unable to solve. For example, should you be located somewhere where we cannot reach you at the point of your death, say over or in water or fire, they will arrive and solve the problem instantly before handing you over to us. They can move with the speed of a superman.

We know you are around and helping us, but are you able to influence us in our decisions or our direction and destiny?

Yes. We can help make some things happen and we can alter certain things. Sometimes, we can also see the future. Unfortunately, though, we are not always able to help. For example, if you were going to have an accident, we may very likely not know. That is because we may not be in contact at that time with the spirit of the person who is going to cause the accident. Only their family spirits would know that and their natural priority would be only for the person they are guiding.

You have mentioned that in the spiritual form you are warm. Is there a special reason for this?

Yes. I use the energy of the warmth to help heal and cure your problems, either alone or with other spirits, or through the psychic healer's help.

With your spiritual energy, are you able to enter or pass through a human being or an animal?

No, this is not possible.

When somebody is dying of an incurable disease and they are suffering, what do you do?

We are very limited in our powers to help someone or save them. However, if they are seriously ill and we cannot bear to watch them with their prolonged suffering any longer, we will try to help take them away into the peace and safety of the spirit world.

When a woman loses her unborn child during pregnancy through a miscarriage, what happens to the spirit of the lost baby?

If a miscarriage occurs, the baby's spirit will wait and then help the second child of the mother if another child is conceived and born. It will follow the second child and help it to be more intelligent where possible. In such cases, the second child may experience what is sometimes called an 'invisible friend.'

Alternatively, the spirit may come back again in the years ahead, but not to the same person or family. It may take up to more than eight hundred years for this to happen. This does not happen if you are the first born and the miscarriage is the second born.

What happens to babies that die at birth?

We try to ensure that all babies are born perfect, but unfortunately this is sometimes difficult to control. We try to make sure that when they come back again, they have a better chance in life.

Why are some people very privileged in this life when there are many others who live in poverty and suffer terrible diseases and pain?

It is all just chance. Even if you are lucky enough to be born into a family with money, you may still contract illness or take the wrong path in life and end up very unhappy. You often hear of young people that are heirs to great fortunes taking their own life and this is often due to drugs, gambling, alcohol, etc, so money does not automatically bring happiness to anyone.

Generally, people make their own luck in life by being kind and considerate to others, working hard and not setting out deliberately to hurt or cheat others in any way. If you do set out to harm others, you may well struggle in life, and if you do, it is usually deserved in some way.

After entering Heaven as a spirit and learning all the things you know, are there any things that you now regret or you wish you had done otherwise before you passed on?

Most spirits have similar thoughts of that kind. They are really quite similar to what were our living thoughts, but even more so. We wish we had said more kind things and done more kind deeds. We see their importance so much more clearly now. Words and thoughts of affection are what many wish they had used more often. Like so many people still living on earth, we wish we had told people more of our love for them before direct contact was lost and it was all too late.

Most, too, would like to have made better financial provisions where we could for our loved ones who still have their earth-lives before them. We feel sad to see them suffer difficulties and financial problems that we might have been able to help. Had we only known that which we know now.

One thing that I often hear mentioned is that leaving the earth without making a proper will can cause such terrible family disagreements later. Great care is needed with things like that. Some spirits, I know, have been very distressed by what has happened to their families.

Will we stay on this planet?

When God decides to leave this planet, He will take all His children with Him and eventually He will return home to the other side of the universe. He cannot take the Earth with Him and we cannot survive here without Him.

Global warming is very worrying for us, as are the continual wars and nuclear risks that threaten to damage the planet and make it uninhabitable. God and His spirits are monitoring the world, but we are hoping that something will be done to remove the carbon from the atmosphere by you humans. If God is forced to abandon the earth because it can no longer sustain human life, He will take the spirits out of your bodies at that moment and take all of us with Him. Anything left that dies after this event would just turn to ash and its spirit would die with it.

When God takes us with Him to the other side of the universe, how will we survive the journey?

He will create a large 'roadway' in the shape of a great energy tunnel to protect us. We are actually looking forward to this day when we can return to see where we originally came from.

Is God proud of His spiritual children?

Yes, very much so because we are uniquely different from other spirits in the universe as we have previously had human form with all the emotions and everything that goes with being human.

Chapter 5

THE UNIVERSE AND PLANET EARTH
Some Puzzling Questions About the
Earth's Past Answered

What can you tell us about the Ice Age?

Contrary to what everyone believes, the Ice Age was the beginning of the planet. Earth arrived here in a frozen state after travelling through the universe. It slowly started to warm and melt as God and His spirits set the planet up, with the volcanoes playing a significant part in determining its structure. This process took billions of years.

Why did dinosaurs become extinct?

There are many reasons for this, including the fact that they ate each other. Dinosaurs also could not breed in large numbers as cats and dogs do, for example. They travelled around alone looking for food, which made them more vulnerable to other predators. This meant that they left their mates to travel and got killed on the way, the mate was left without a mature partner to breed with. The real problem was the lack of an adequate food chain for dinosaurs. As the dinosaur population dwindled, God sought other avenues to produce His spirits from.

The older spirits say that the dinosaur came before its time and that their spines and bone structure were badly designed. They were often too big and clumsy to be efficient animals. There were not as many dinosaurs in the world as was held to be and they were only found in certain parts of the world. They did not die in an ice age as this was before their time. The preserved remains that are found from time to time trapped as fossils are due to climate changes.

What came before the monkeys and gorillas, and how did we develop?

At one stage, God tried to develop the human being from extremely large birds, but they had very prominent chest areas. They did not survive because they could not breed very well. They were also too big, clumsy and easily caught and were therefore preyed upon by other animals. They evolved from the sea. They had a monkey-like face and monkey and bird hair. They had legs and feet like a human with long toes.

God thought He could develop this life form into what would be a human being that could fly, but they had trouble taking off and found it difficult to hide from predators. He then decided to follow the path of the monkey and the gorilla.

The more primitive gorilla-like creatures started to reach up for food from the ground and slowly developed into man. At that time, we were very small, but we gradually grew taller and although it may seem strange, both reaching for our food and dancing encouraged an increase our height. We were originally frightened to leave the protection of the dense jungles. However, when we did, we went different ways and our bare feet played an important part in developing the structure of our brain.

Over the next two million years, mankind developed different characteristics according to where they lived, whether it was colour, habits, language or height. Remember that we still wear make-up and hang beads around our necks, arms and ankles. This all stems from the more primitive stages of our life in the jungle.

Is the planet Earth over-populated?

Generally not, but the planet is over-populated in certain continents and countries and this is affecting the food chains around the world.

Will we ever live on the moon?

Men will continue to visit the moon, but will never live on it. It has the same problem as the earth, but is smaller. If you start messing about with its delicate balance by shifting weight around on it, it will move and that in turn could cause it to fall out of the orbit around the earth and float away.

This is an extreme example of what could happen, but the lesser problem could be damage to the planet earth and the earth's tides. The money now spent on exploratory trips to the moon would be better spent in the prevention of pollution on Earth or in trying to rebalance the earth.

What is the black hole?

It is like a giant vacuum that sucks in the gases, the rocks and other matter, cleans them and recycles them again to other parts of the universe. It feeds on rubbish and it is spiritually alive. There are hundreds of them in space, we do not know exactly how many, and they move around cleaning the universe. They grow bigger over time, but they are not dangerous. Nobody has ever been there, but this is what the scientists here in the spirit world believe.

Scientists believe that the super, massive black holes are the gravitational centre of each galaxy and that the stars and planets revolve around them. Is this theory true?

These are just bigger black holes that grow over time. They are alive in the sense that they are energy. If they were to blow up and spread out through the galaxy, another black hole would absorb them.

Why did the Romans kill Druids?

There were a few famous episodes like the time when they were looking for five Druids who were thieves and had raped local women. They could not identify the individuals concerned and were afraid that the rapes would continue. Therefore, the Romans killed all of the Druids they could find to ensure that there were no more rapes.

Chapter 6

THE SPIRIT WORLD'S CONCERN FOR
EARTH AND ITS ENVIRONMENT

I know you have given us many answers, ideas and hints, but what are the spirits' underlying reasons for this contact and activity at just this time?

The spirit world is doubly alarmed now at the destructive effects of global warming that are coming with its resulting world-wide flooding storms and terrible droughts. The degree of destruction and the huge death toll is unimaginable to you. It will be beyond dreadful.

Firstly, we are alarmed because of the effects of all this in decreasing the future population of mankind. It is our task to look after the human race and your actions are going to hinder us from doing that properly. Secondly, we are alarmed as this is our planet and home too and its damage will seriously affect us. We are therefore making this contact in order to advise people everywhere what steps can be taken before it's too late.

You must restore the planet to normality. We hope our messages through these contacts and the book will now reach the people and the leaders of all nations stressing the desperate need for rapid help whatever the costs may be. Moving huge masses of oil out of the earth and the weight changes from the melting ice caps is destabilising everything.

To prove our integrity and the urgency of our warnings, even to non-believers, we spirits have given you answers to many of the past and present myths and mysteries of the world. We have explained or corrected stories about the events and characters from the Bible as witnessed by older spirits who were actually present at those times.

Through this book, you will learn where we all came from, why we are here, where we are going and the very purpose of our lives. It is our responsibility to look after you and it is your responsibility to look after the planet.

Why do we have so many climate problems now?

We have seen a lot of flooding in recent times and this is due to the way in which the world is being mistreated by humans. You have to start treating the planet with the love, the care and the respect that it deserves. This is very important to the spirit world too, as many of our loved ones are still living humans and we do not want to lose any of you. We all want to live harmoniously together whether it is as spirits or as humans.

The countries that are destroying the planet will soon be targeted by God's own spirits and will suffer first. Bridges will fall. There will be floods and fires, and much heartache for the people of those countries. The land that has been reclaimed from the sea over time will be taken back by it.

At the present rate it will take up to ten years before the various nations and their leaders start to realise what is really happening. And you don't have ten years available. Currently, the world as you know it is over-populated by man and the balance of man to animal may have to be restored. God's own spirits have stated that they are trying to put things back into balance. We are all sad about this as our own loved ones may suffer in the process. Man needs to respect the land and the sea and stop polluting the planet.

Currently, man is just taking everything out of the earth, such as oil and other minerals. With ice melting in the polar regions, the weight and pressure is moving around and making the planet unbalanced and therefore unstable. This upset balance is even more disturbed by the loss of the weight of the huge amounts of oil being pumped out of some areas.

When this is burned to gases that cannot be returned into the ground, the balance of the planet is obviously affected. You also need to start treating seawater so that it can be used for drinking and also for plants and crops.

By late in 2008, you will have seen some terrible things starting and you will understand more about what I am trying to tell you. America will have more big storms than they have ever had before and there will be more strong winds and hurricanes than previously experienced ever before. This is what I am being told in the spirit world and what they believe will happen.

There is hotter weather coming everywhere in the world and it will create chaos all around the world. America and China will suffer terrible floods and there will also be many minor earthquakes in the next ten years as well as several very serious ones. Some of these earthquakes will be in places that have never had such problems before. Places that are prone to minor earthquakes will see much more serious ones. Due to the shifting and movement of the planet, more cracks will appear in the Earth's surface as a result of its imbalance.

Why do we have so many climate problems now?

This planet does not just belong to people who are now alive. We spirits live here too. We must protect it for our own sakes as well as for the sake of our loved ones and families. The spirit world is taking action now,.. this little book is part of that action. Men and spirits should work together but be sure, if man does not co-operate we shall act both alone and with the help of the Heavenly Spirits.

This then is our vital message… ACT NOW.

What does the future hold for the human population?

We cannot predict the future accurately so far ahead in time, but unless something drastic happens to change the present destruction of the planet, the human population will be more than halved during the next century.

Densely populated areas near to rivers and coastlines will be submerged. Many millions of people will die by drowning, fevers, starvation or the plagues that will be caused by the huge numbers of decaying bodies which will not have been disposed of properly.

In some places, the air will be too polluted to breathe safely. This will cause breathing difficulties to millions of people so that they will become more susceptible to other diseases that will sweep the earth. AIDS, tuberculosis and other infectious diseases will destroy vast sections of the human population all around the world.

You must avoid and minimise pollution in order to save the planet and enable mankind to survive. And you must do this right now. There is not a moment to lose. Address the matter of carbon emissions and stop destroying the rain forests. Most importantly of all, stop taking the oil out of the earth.

The large quantities of oil that are being pumped out and burned are lost into the atmosphere. Not only has this lightened the weight of the earth, but more significantly, it has started to unbalance it and has affected the vibrations on its axis. This, in turn, has also affected the weather around the world, as we have seen throughout the year 2007.

You've not experienced anything much yet. There is far, far worse – immeasurably worse, to come. In other words, the delicate balance of the earth is being disturbed and is at the mercy of the sun and moon. This is something that scientists do not yet seem to have realised – that an imbalance of the Earth by removing weight in the form of oil and the ice caps from some places and not counterbalancing it in others is a dreadfully dangerous practice.

At the same time, the rain forests that have been a major part of combating the carbon dioxide levels are being stripped daily at a dangerously high rate. This, in turn, is making pollution worse. In a short time, maybe less forty years time or even sooner, the air will be so polluted that humans will not be able to breathe properly. It is already happening in some badly affected areas of the world.

Is this the legacy that you wish to leave our children?

There is so much that can be done both to combat

pollution and to address global warming that is not being done by world leaders or even individuals. We are surprised that it is not yet every individual's top priority for the future and the future of their children and grandchildren. It is the biggest threat of all by miles. It's far more important than bothering about fuel supplies and terrorism and things like that. Why can't you all see it?

Are you concerned about the pollution of the planet?

We believe that mankind will find a solution to global warming. As we have already told you, we hope the problem will be solved before the ice caps melt. You must all look after the planet for all our sakes.

What is the importance of fish and human fishing methods?

If nature, as controlled by God's heavenly spirits, believed that fish were going to suffer as a result of what is happening on Earth and the mismanagement of the planet, then the land would be destroyed first rather than the seas.

The fish were God's first important creatures and they have a special place with Him. They are also a complete food chain, which means that if the animal kingdom was destroyed, God, with His own heavenly spirits, could recreate it again from the fish in the sea.

So, do we over-farm the fish?

You should give certain areas of the world's oceans, rivers and streams, etc, an eight to ten-year break from fishing to allow the fish to breed and replenish the waters. It is also important that their own food chain is replenished for the good of the world.

What type of fuel will we use in the future?

There are plenty of kinds, like nuclear and renewable fuel. But oil will be needed for a long time because so many machines are built to run on it. A sort of hybrid bean plant will soon be developed by cross-breeding two other kinds. That will produce a very oily plant with a kind of nut or bean fruit that will be crushed for the oil. It's a kind of bio-fuel, I suppose.

Discovery of this is not far away and, compared with fossil oils, it will be relatively cheap to grow and process. The beans themselves are skin coloured and the ends of the beans are green. There will be thousands of beans growing on one single plant.

Have you any other ideas for harnessing energy?

Yes, we see in the future much more use of tidal and wave power and of wind – windmill power. We can see every house having one windmill or more. To make them blend in with the environment, we can see them all painted different rainbow colours. But whether we like them or not, we will have to put up with them or go without their energy.

Do you think governments world-wide should set an example with regard to global warming?

Yes, they could start by turning the lights off in government offices at night. They should also turn all the lights out on roads after about 2.00 am. After that, road users should go slower and use their own lights. Cats' eyes should be everywhere. Many traffic lights should be replaced by roundabouts. Efficient solar power should be developed even for countries where amounts of sunlight are low. There has to be a reasonable compromise between the convenience of energy use and the protection of our planet.

How can we help the world?

Take great care of the countryside. Stop over-fishing; give the fish a chance to breed and restock the oceans and rivers. Plant fruit trees everywhere to feed the hungry. Try to keep the water clean and, where you can, try to prevent cruelty in the world wherever possible.

Do the spirits have a general message for humans?

Whatever happens in our life on Earth as human beings, whether it be happy, sad, fearful or tragic, it is all very important. It is all part of the learning process that we go through in our lifetime. Throughout our lives, we build on our personal experiences and are better people for many of the things that happen to us.

We entered the physical world through the first tunnel – our mother's birth canal – and have all the feelings, emotions and intelligence that a young animal would have. The physical body and the young spirit grow together throughout our younger years. Our bodies generally mature by the age of twenty-one years or even younger in some individuals, but our spirit matures at about the age of twenty-seven years.

At the time of our death, our spirit then discards its

earthly body which is no longer needed and passes through the second tunnel in order to enter into Heaven, the kingdom of God. During our earthly life, we produce more children who, in turn, will follow our path towards enlarging God's spiritual kingdom.

Although Heaven extends from the Earth's surface to the highest mountain tops, most of the active spirits stay on the lower levels to look after their loved ones in the earthly world.

If you die before your twenty-seventh birthday, you will come to heaven to wait for your second human life. In your second life, the spirits will try to ensure that you live a longer life.

Once you reach the age of twenty-seven years old, God considers you to be a fully developed mature earth spirit. Once you pass over after this age, no matter what age you may be, you are not expected to return in human form again. Instead, you will find the true and unbelievable eternal happiness that we all experience here in Heaven.

Once you have been to Heaven, there are not many spirits who would wish for any further earthly lives. There is no way that I would personally ever want to go back through the tunnel and become human again. Life as a spirit here in Heaven is so much better than life as a human being. That is our overall message of hope and comfort to those still alive and who face such horrors in the years to come. Be sure that there is an end to it; it is a happy end… and one day you will come into the peace and love of Heaven.

Chapter 7

PSYCHIC MATTERS AND CONNECTIONS

How do spirits appear to a psychic or clairvoyant?

They may appear as an orb of light, a small spherical light that shows the spirit's energy. From time to time, these orbs of light may appear to others and even may show up in photographs when they wish to be seen by non-psychics. At other times, they can appear looking just as they were during their life as a human being.

When a clairvoyant has a client in front of them and is about to give them a reading, do their family spirits have any knowledge that this is going to happen?

If someone books an appointment or even just walks in off the street, their family spirits will already know that this was going to happen. They may well know as much as six weeks before the person plans to consult the clairvoyant, even if the person concerned does not know at that stage.

The spirit family would know the exact day and time that the reading was going to happen. This is important because then not only will the immediate guardian spirit from the family be there, but also other family and, maybe, friends and acquaintances who have passed over will also come. They may well all want to have a chance to be helpful or to communicate through a clairvoyant.

Can a person learn to be psychic?

You have to be born with the gift. You cannot teach someone to become a psychic. It is a gift that is often found in families and usually passed down through them. Sometimes people do not know that they even possess this wonderful gift; they have to be told about it by another psychic. If you have the gift, you will come realise it over time by the things that you see and feel that others do not. That is how Wilf learned about his gift and started to develop it.

We all dream at night. What is a dream and does it have any significance to our lives?

These happen when the brain is unloading memories or thoughts or events that have recently taken place. Your brain is always unloading its recent memories of events, situations and worries by using the dream route. The information is being sent for storage in the brain's memory.

As this information flashes through the subconscious – that is sleeping parts of the brain – fragments that often appear disjointed and distorted briefly appear in the forefront of the mind. That is why dreams often seem so twisted and mixed up and with events seeming to come together that are out of sequence and without any obvious sensible meaning.

However, you can also dream into the future. Often this is when we are trying to talk to you through your spirit. When you have a nightmare, it is your spirit not wanting to accept the dream. It then tries to divert the dream or cover it with other emotions. It will seem distorted because you are not getting the entire dream, but only disjointed parts.

When you are asleep, we can always talk to your spirit. Your dreams are your thoughts and we spirits can easily come into them. This is one of the reasons you dream so much about people from your family and friends who have passed on to become spirits. It's worth realising that... that we are really there with you as you dream.

Sometimes if you wake up shouting, screaming or whimpering or you find you cannot seem to wake up properly, this is because your spirit has left your body for a while and has not yet returned in time for when you awaken. Remember that your physical brain and your spirit are entirely different things. Your brain might be wanting to wake up, but your spirit is not ready to re-enter your body. Therefore, your brain has to wait.

It may be that your spirit has gone ahead in time and you think you are dreaming. That is the explanation of déjà-vu, for example, when you think that you have been down a certain road before. That is because your spirit has been previously to that place and your brain is getting an overflow of memories as if it were your physical body that had been there.

Will time travel ever be possible?

No, this is totally impossible even for human spirits. Sometimes, we can see into the future as far as an individual's life-span goes. We can also assist with setting the path you take in the future, but neither we nor anyone nor anything else can change the past.

A vortex, in paranormal terms, is a manifestation of energy that is associated with ghosts and spirits, and is also considered as a possible gateway into the spirit world. Do vortices really exist, and if so, what is their function?

These are the spiritual energy tunnels that God has placed all around the world. Normally they cannot be seen or photographed and are used by spirits to travel at high speeds from one place to another. When a photograph has been successfully taken of these tunnels, it is always because there was a ghost inside, not just of the tunnels themselves.

Pyrokinesis is a very rare psychic ability that some individuals possess and allows them to set fire to an object without making contact with it. Is it possible?

It is a manifestation of the gift of the healing power that some people possess, but do not yet realise that they have it. Consequently, such people may sometimes have too much of this healing energy and it then comes out through their hands as a form of heat. The spirit in their body also holds an excess of energy and they are able to let this go and become released. An average person who is without healing powers will need all of their available energy to just exist.

Automatic writing is claimed by some to be a method of spiritual communication sometimes performed by a medium. It is believed by others to be just the result of the writer's own subconsciousness. Could you please explain the facts?

This is a gift that is given to some people, again such as Wilf or others with psychic or clairvoyant abilities have. It is a gift from the spirit world and is where the spirits work through your hand for the relaying of important messages.

If you are blessed with this gift, you should use it and no harm will come to anyone with it or to those for whom it is used. It is a gift that any spirit can give to a human being, perhaps to help them and their family.

What are ley lines? There are many theories relating to them suggesting they are sources of energy from the earth itself and that spirits draw energy from them. Is this true?

It is often believed that these are powerful earth energy sources, but they are nothing more than a form of telling the time and navigation. The spirits do not draw energy from them.

Does extra-sensory perception (ESP) really exist?

ESP is dealt with by a part of the brain that is not normally used by everyone. It is similar to clairvoyance, and only a small proportion of the world's population has this ability. Psychics, who are in the minority, also have a similar area of the brain that is well developed for us spirits to tune into.

What about palmistry?

This was the first ever method of predicting the future and it is a method that will carry on forever.

It can be very accurate at times, but it can also be very misleading. This is especially so if it is done by individuals who do not really know what they are doing, don't understand the workings of the spirit world or are not genuinely in contact with the spirit world at all. A clairvoyant who has the gift can read a palm, but it is the spirit belonging to the subject who will really be doing the work and providing the information.

Do our birth dates and star signs relate to our personalities?

Yes, very much so. However this too can also be very misleading at times as our individual traits may merely come from our close family rather than relating to our birth sign. Generally, though, the time, place and season of birth and then its association with birthdays, festivities, weather, hours of daylight and so on can influence the developing mind and personality. It's not the actual stars themselves that do it. This is why we should take birth signs into account when choosing friends and life partners.

Do the spirits put any value on the star signs?

Yes, they can be very helpful to humans when assessed properly by gifted astrologers. It is not so much the actual star sign that is important, but the physical time of year which has influenced the conception and makeup of the individual. Even the time of day that a person is born can affect an individual's personality, as it often does in twins and brothers and sisters born around the same times. Also the time within the span of the star sign influences the individual's personality.

You often hear about people being born on the cusp. This is when they are born right at the end of one star sign and on the verge of the next one. They may have predominant traits that relate to one sign or the other, or even both.

Should we use a ouija board to contact spirits?

No. There are many mischievous spirits in the spirit world, which is fun for us, but not for you. Ouija boards are dangerous, particularly if they get into the wrong hands. Spirits passing by at the time may try to contact you because they have no-one else to talk to. You may be lucky to contact one of your loved ones, but often you will get a roaming or frankly malevolent spirit and the consequences may be most unpleasant and unnerving.

Mischievous spirits may intervene and say false or irrelevant things that will never happen and this may frighten you. We still have mischievous children and people who have become earthly spirits who like to joke and laugh. Everyone is welcome here, but the behaviour of some can be less correct than we might wish.

Do poltergeists really exist?

Spirits can pick up and throw very light objects such as a cup, a towel or a sheet, but they cannot lift items of furniture such as chairs, tables, etc. We would certainly never attempt to break glass or similar items as this may hurt people.

In many cases, stories about evil spirits and poltergeists are just made up because the people concerned want to move from the house they are living in. Haunting by ghosts is often the excuse they will give to local councils and to some private landlords. In many instances, they are large families in council houses and they just use this as an excuse to try to move elsewhere for personal reasons. It is very rare that you will find such stories relating to families in houses that they both occupy and own.

Where do flying saucers come from?

They are the heavenly spirits that are just visible for moments. These spirits are moving around the Earth constantly and they are controlling everything. They are pure energy and when they travel, they take a shape similar to that which you call a flying saucer. They are very fast, mostly too fast to be seen, but can still be seen when they are motionless.

Does the spontaneous combustion of humans really ever happen and if so, how?

This is all to do with bone structure and body makeup. When they are born, some people have the ability to absorb and retain larger amounts of phosphorus than are wanted or needed in the body. This may be worsened by a mother eating the wrong foods during her pregnancy. As the person grows, the phosphorus builds up and remains mostly in the marrow of the bones until eventually, under the right conditions, it ignites and causes the whole body to burn until it is nothing other than ashes.

Can teleportation, the psychic transportation of an object from one place to another, really happen?

I feel that this is totally impossible and will never happen! I have never witnessed it myself. Nor have any other spirits told me of it happening and I have asked many about it.

When a woman has twins or triplets, is there any spiritual connection to a multiple birth?

Where there have been tragedies or accidents in the past, for example when a family has died together on the same day, in some cases their spirits may come back together as a multiple birth. However, this can take many, many years to happen. It is very rare that they come from the family of those having the multiple birth. Frequently, they return in this form if any or all of them were under the age of twenty-seven years at the time of their death.

What is the phenomenon of hypnotism?

Hypnotism is a practitioner talking directly to the brain and bypassing the spiritual or thinking self. The brain listens to the hypnotist's commands instead of its spirit's commands. The brain can be likened to a computer in this respect. Hypnosis is a useful method of treatment for many conditions.

Can we be 'cursed' by man or a spirit?

No. There are no powers in the spirit world or on earth that can curse or cause ill health or ill will to humans. It does not matter what someone has done or what has happened, no-one can curse them.

What happens if a person is cruel to others?

When someone is very cruel to other human beings and takes pleasure from their actions, they may be accepted into Heaven through their own spiritual family's decision to forgive them. We, however, will punish them in our own way when they are here and keep moving them on so that they are not allowed to be at rest or to be near their loved ones and friends. However, some of us spirits are more forgiving than others. Consequently, this punishment may not be so severe in certain families.

Can ghosts harm us?

Over the generations, people have adopted the view that ghosts can harm you and that they might use their powers to move small objects. However, they will not use their powers to harm you in any way. They would only move these small objects to make you aware that they are there and would like to be just left alone.

Dowsing is the ancient art of locating water or metals with a Y-shaped stick or two rods. Does this really work and how?

Yes, and not only for water and metals. This is a natural method of finding water used over many years. Originally, the apes and gorillas adopted this method to find water and insects to eat. They even learned how to suck the water or insects out through a hollow bamboo cane.

This method of searching for water was carried on through many, many generations. It works very well with a metal rod because the metal will attract the water and vice versa. Skilled dowsers can also use the method to find other things.

Chapter 8

FAMOUS PEOPLE AND THEIR STORIES

Adolf Hitler (1889-1945) is probably the most hated man in history. There are lots of rumours about his death and did he or did he not escape? How did he die and where is his spirit now?

He died by his own hand. His spirit is still trapped in the ruins of the bunker where he died in Berlin. This is because his family of spirits that passed on to Heaven both before and after his death are ashamed of him and the suffering that he caused both to his own people and to many others. Consequently, they will not yet allow him to progress into Heaven as he would like to do. By stopping him from using the tunnel to Heaven, they are able to keep him trapped in the bunker where he died as a punishment for his sins.

Elizabeth I (1533-1601) is usually referred to as 'The Virgin Queen.' Did she really die as a Virgin Queen?

No. She had had several lovers during her lifetime. She was a clever woman, but had a dislike of making decisions. She also did not like people walking towards her, so she always insisted that people approach her from the side if at all possible because of this phobia.

At one point in her younger days, she accidentally became pregnant. However, because she wanted other foreign kings and nobles to think she may marry at some time in the future and use the marriage to form a political alliance with another country, she realised that she could not have the child. She felt she had to get rid of the baby, which she did. It's not surprising that this affected her emotionally for a very long time.

She never felt able to get married as it meant that the truth would come out that she was not a virgin and that she had had secret affairs. Such things were not the behaviour that was expected of a person of her rank and position. She made up for all this by having a succession of partners, not all of them noblemen.

Napoleon Bonaparte (1769-1821) was a great military leader who managed to conquer most of Europe and went on to become Emperor of the French. He was later captured by the British and imprisoned on the island of St Helena, where he died in mysterious circumstances. How did he die?

Napoleon had stomach cancer and whatever that might have done to him later, this was not what killed him at the time. He was a strong man with great willpower and the cancer would probably have taken a long time to kill him. The leaders of the other countries that had been at war with both Napoleon and France were always afraid that he might try to escape again as he had before. They felt he would be able to build another army, particularly as he was a military expert with a genius for strategy and command, and this would inevitably cause them further problems.

Therefore, the leaders plotted against Napoleon and poisoned him as well as other members of his family that they felt may also be harmful in the future. His wife, who was also a princess, was not poisoned as they felt that she would be more valuable to them in helping to maintain peace both in Europe and in other parts of the world.

Napoleon was given several doses of a poison that caused him a very painful death with a strong sensation of burning in his stomach and bones. It was very unpleasant and caused his body to be distorted and ugly. This is one of the reasons for Napoleon's spirit not wanting his tomb to be opened.

The Grand Duchess Anastasia Nicolaieva (1901-1918) was the youngest daughter of the last Czar, and her parents were Nicholas II and Alexandra Romanov of Russia. Did she die on 16th July, 1918, the same day that her family were killed, or did she survive and live under an assumed name as has been rumoured?

She was not killed at the same time as the rest of her family, but kept alive because the new government thought she knew where the family treasures had been hidden. They kept her alive for a further twelve days until they had found the family's gold, jewellery and diamonds. She never told them how and where to find the treasure, but they found out from servants and others.

Anastasia's spirit has told us that it was believed at that time that the diamonds were cursed and that was why they never did those who stole them any good. Of course, the idea of being cursed is just an old wives' tale as there is no such thing.

Amelia Earhart (1897-1937) was the first woman to fly solo across the Atlantic in 1937. The same year she also attempted to fly around the world. During this flight, her plane vanished with her and her co-pilot on board. No wreckage was ever found. What really happened?

Her aeroplane developed a fuel problem and got taken off course before the fuel all ran out. She got thrown out of it at quite a height over the sea when the plane suddenly took a nosedive and fell out of the sky. She had always said that she would never crash the plane.

The plane was heading towards a crash landing over land, but it nosedived and ditched into the sea. The co-pilot was still on board at the time and he also perished in the crash.

Nostradamus (1503-1566) wrote a lot of things that predicted the future. Was he really able to do this and, if so, how?

He had a psychic gift and received his predictions from staring out at and beyond the stars. He saw a lot of things, but did not understand them fully and therefore did not know how to explain them. That is why so much of what he wrote is both vague and in riddles. Only about a quarter of his predications are or ever will be found accurate.

King Arthur (fifth century) is a legendary king of England. What is the truth about him?

Arthur was a stocky man of about 5ft 9ins tall, which was tall for those days, and very handsome. As a child, he was bought up with a great deal of violence due to his mixing constantly with soldiers from his father's army. His father had an army of forty men, and for Arthur's safety, he was always moved from one place to another.

From a young age, he was taught to fight with a sword and continued to develop his sword skills throughout his childhood and teenage years. However, he was not a very skilful swordsman and preferred to rely on his brute strength.

His father died when he was only eighteen years old, after which he was ceremonially presented with the royal sword known as Excalibur, which was in his family and had been passed down through several generations. It was a well-made sword which had killed and injured many people, and Arthur believed it was meant to prove that he was a man. However, it did not make him a man and he has realised that now.

Following his father's death, it was a symbolic ritual in their society in those days for the successor to show that he was now in charge of the realm and the army, and that he was the new leader of the men and the people. Arthur was therefore confirmed as being in command of his father's army, castle and other possessions. He did not remove the sword from the stone as the legend says. This was just a story that Arthur made up himself in order to boast about his magic and strength.

Arthur loved his family very much, but because he was separated from them at such a young age, it affected him later on in his adult life. He learnt to deal with this pain by putting his family to the back of his mind by using selective memories. His family did not desert him, but he was kept at a distance away from them for reasons of his own safety. His sisters were on a totally different wavelength to Arthur and he could not understand them – or they him – as they spoke a different language from him. They were very loving towards Arthur. This he found very difficult to cope with as he had never received such affection before and was not able to return it.

Arthur was unable to sleep more than an average of two to three hours per night, and always had a sword and a dagger beside him. He did not trust anyone, especially the officers from his army. Arthur knew that they could turn on him at any time, even just for money. He loved his dogs and horses, and was never cruel to them. Money was no object when it came to his animals. He loved food, and his favourite meal was meat.

Arthur was not a real king. Neither was his father. They were the equivalent to a Lord of the Manor. Arthur inherited Tintagel Castle in Cornwall, England, from his father, who had captured it peacefully years some before along with all the servants that lived and worked there. Both there and elsewhere the army kept horses for their own use and for breeding as horses were required due to the amount of travelling they did.

Arthur's wealth was accumulated by growing crops and selling them, and also by extracting taxes from businesses and villages nearby. As the years passed, Arthur's army decreased in size to only twenty-eight soldiers as some had been killed and others had left him or grown old. Arthur still had to pay and feed them and did so, even though they were paid only a pittance.

Arthur offered the protection services of these paid troops to the surrounding villages so they would not be molested by raiders and other potential enemies.

He imposed a big levy or tax on this service. This amounted to an early form of taxation for his protection services.

Arthur was a rogue who enjoyed battles and fighting. Except for his attacks against Danes and invading pirates, the people Arthur fought were not professional fighters as such, but were generally farmers and peasants. He had a very good strategic mind when it came to battles and could work out the best way to launch an attack or ambush or to raid villages without many of his soldiers being injured.

Arthur was very kind to his own people, but was very cruel to outsiders and would rather fight and frighten them off than talk to them. It was not his fault, as it was just the way he had been brought up on the road with an army from a young age. Arthur lived by the sword and felt he would also die by the sword. This was the only life that he knew and was comfortable with.

His grandfather was good at telling stories and often told them to Arthur when he was a young boy. He inherited this ability from his grandfather and learned a lot about the world and its events beyond Cornwall due to his interest in the world around him because of the stories that he was told.

Arthur was attracted to girls who had long black hair and dark eyes. He fell in love with a lady he could not have and loved her so much it hurt. However, he soon realised that his love was not reciprocated and felt foolish.

Merlin was Arthur's best friend and had always been a friend of the family. In reality, he behaved more like an older brother to Arthur than a friend. Merlin gave Arthur good advice whenever he could, but was not a magician as has always been thought.

He was just a clever person who knew many things for the times that he lived in. Very few people liked Merlin and because of this he was afraid to leave the castle on his own. Through informers, he gathered information for Arthur about which villages to attack and plunder. Merlin was also a very good cook and often prepared meals for Arthur.

He was a kind person, but was also very selfish at the same time. He liked young girls' company and often had more than one around him, but never assaulted or harmed them. He liked the young girls around him as he had no close family of his own who were still alive. However, he did not want boys around him.

Arthur promised that the Castle of Tintagel would be in Merlin's control when he died, but Merlin had two major problems with this. First of all, Arthur would not put anything down on paper, which meant that there was no record of this, just Arthur's promise to Merlin.

Secondly, that he was a man of peace and would not fight to retain possession of the castle. Merlin's spirit still remains at the castle as he feels safe there. He told me that he did go to Heaven for a time, but that he prefers to be in and around his castle, which he still believes is rightfully his. The 'Knights of the Round Table' were Arthur's higher-ranking officers from his army, but they were not real knights.

In Arthur's latter years, he suffered from arthritis in his right ankle, which meant that he was unable to defend either himself or Queen Guinevere adequately and it was this that brought about their deaths. Arthur was killed outside the castle, and the raiders captured the castle and took Queen Guinevere prisoner. They later beheaded her.

Arthur was only forty-two years old when he died. Guinevere was not a queen either by blood or marriage; she was just Arthur's long-term lover. Merlin managed to escape the attack and eventually died at the age of sixty-two years.

Arthur stays by his grave and is very happy there. He loves flowers, and there are many by his grave, which is one reason why he stays there. Arthur spoke to me when I visited his grave and said he wished that he had been more satisfied with what he had when he was alive. He could have been wealthier, but wished that he had paid more attention to his family and friends.

Diana, Princess of Wales (1961-1997) was one of the most loved of all the British royal family. She was tragically killed in a car crash along with her lover, Dodi Fayed, in Paris in an underpass. Many have said that she was killed by the British Secret Service, and others claim that the car was going too fast in trying to escape the paparazzi. What really happened?

Both Princess Diana and Dodi explained to me that the driver of the car was going much too fast. Initially, the car was travelling at a reasonable speed. They were very happy and laughing and joking in the back of the car. The driver then told them that they were being tailed by the press and asked Diana and Dodi if they wanted him to go faster and to try and lose them. They told the driver not to take any avoiding action and then he turned around to speak directly to them to ask if they were sure if they wanted to run the risk of more press photos.

The next thing that they knew was the driver shouting a warning to them and the car shot forward as if someone had jammed a foot down on the accelerator. The car swerved from the road and crashed into the wall of the tunnel. Princess Diana looked around to see what was happening. She heard a great bang… and that was it. She remembers coming around three times due to the efforts of the medical teams, but on the fourth attempt, she went to Heaven as she was too tired and injured to carry on struggling.

It was just a freak accident. The driver could not release his foot in time to avoid what happened. There was nothing more to it than that. All the talk and theories about murder and trying to pin the blame on Prince Charles and the Royal Family are nothing but nonsense. Princess Diana told me that Prince Charles was in no way to blame for the accident as he loved her in his own strange way and would never have harmed the mother of his children.

Princess Diana also admitted that she had pushed Prince Charles out of the marriage after the birth of her second son, Prince Harry. She explained that the reason for that was that he became very old and staid in his ways. She said that she, on the other hand, felt that she still was very young and was enjoying the limelight that she was in and the life that she led. Prince Charles loved his children dearly and at that time, just after the birth of Prince Harry, would never have done anything that would break up the marriage. He had his own interests: that was all. The age gap widened between Diana and Charles and caused a rift in the marriage that could not be healed.

Dodi Fayed (1955-1997) was the lover of Princess Diana and he died with her in a car crash in a Paris underpass. Does he have anything further to add about the crash?

Dodi said that he was in the back of the car with Princess Diana and her bodyguard was sat in the front alongside the driver. There were press following on motorbikes, and there was also a car following. Dodi said that he was joking around and laughing with Diana in the back of the car, and that they were acting like a pair of schoolchildren. They were in love, and that is what you do when you are in the early days of a new romance and love affair as they were, he said.

The following bikes were getting closer to the car, so the driver turned around and asked them if they wanted him to go faster. They answered saying they did not want to go any faster. Unfortunately, as the driver turned around, his foot got stuck on the accelerator pedal and the car suddenly shot forward. As a result of this, the car swerved off the road and hit a pillar of the underpass.

Dodi said that no-one killed either of them and that it was just an accident. He thought that the driver was probably at fault and to blame for the crash due to the fact that he turned around and then lost control of the car. Essentially, it was bad judgement on the driver's part, but it was also a freak accident.

Both Diana and Dodi blame themselves for laughing and joking around in the back of the car, and feel that this may have distracted the driver. Also they feel that the accident was probably a combination of both their fault and the driver's fault for looking around as he did rather than keeping his eyes on the road. Princess Diana is adamant that both she and Dodi do not blame anyone except themselves for what happened.

They are both in the spirit world together now and are very happy and spend time with each other nearly every other day. It is not possible for them to see each other every day because they each want to see and be with their own families, too. In particular, Diana wants to be with her sons, the Princes William and Harry, as they grow up and make their way in life.

Both Diana and Dodi told me that they had a wonderful but short time together, and because of the timing of the accident so soon after they had met and fallen in love, their relationship had not fully blossomed.

Diana used to tell Dodi about Prince Charles and their time together and how people blamed him for the divorce because he had an affair with his first love, Camilla Parker-Bowles. However, it was not like that in reality, as their love gradually died away following the birth of their second son.

Charles followed his family's wishes that he marry Diana, but he never really had a great passion for her, although he did love her in his own way. His upbringing also contributed to his lack of passion and his coldness in life, but they still both believe he would never have left Diana. However, she pushed him out by being cold towards him and keeping him at arm's length emotionally.

Chapter 9

AMERICAN MYSTERIES EXPLAINED

For centuries, there have been alleged sightings of what are called the Brown Mountain Lights in North Carolina, USA. These multi-coloured, sphere-shaped lights move around together and seem to dance. There are many theories attached to this phenomenon, ranging from UFOs to the effects of electrical lightening. To date, this mystery has remained unsolved, so what is the cause?

They are very strong spirits returning to their burial ground. Brown Mountain is a very spiritual place, and if you are sick, you should go there for healing. They used to take the sick and dying to the ridge, as they thought that by taking them up higher, it would help them on their way to Heaven. The spirits are good and the different colours seen at certain times of the year are the colours of their energies.

The 'Philadelphia Experiment' is supposed to have taken place aboard the ship USS Eldbridge in 1943. Witnesses claim that the ship was made invisible and also that it had been physically teleported to Norfolk in Virginia and later back again. The crew became ill and some died shortly after leaving the harbour. It was also claimed that the crew could walk through walls. Is there any truth in all this and what is the real explanation?

A very strong radar system with a large beam was put onto the ship. Due to the power of the radar, a mist formed and the ship was hidden behind it. The radar affected the crew on board the ship and some died suddenly, causing the ship to go off-course. Basically, it was like a strong force field, and the radar system was put onto the ship to see what would happen and if it would make it invisible to other radar systems elsewhere in the world.

This experiment was also very frightening for the spirit world, and when the US government tried to repeat the experiment later, the earthly spirits ensured that it went wrong and was given up.

During the Second World War, many pilots reported seeing coloured balls of light in the sky. There were many sightings of these so-called 'Foo Fighters' both over Europe and the Pacific. The mystery is still unsolved, but some have claimed they were experiments that were being carried out for warfare. Others think they were UFO phenomena.

There were two types of balls of light. One was just small meteorites that had entered the Earth's orbit and were burning up. The second type was small particles of damaged plane parts that were caught up in the Earth's currents and were burning and revolving.

The 'Marfa Lights' are mysterious dancing lights that appear around the Mitchell Flats near the town of Marfa in West Texas, USA. They appear to dance and come in different colours and sizes, and seem to have the ability to change colour very rapidly. They have actually been accredited to swamp gas or, yet again, to a UFO phenomenon. What are they really?

This is an uncanny phenomenon that only occurs in three places in the world, all of them very spiritual places due to their position. These lights are God's heavenly spirits playing and this can only be seen at certain times. It is not we earthly spirits, though sometimes we do travel there to see this happen.

I will be going for the first time when it happens next around January or February 2008. I'm told it is a wonderful sight and if you are lucky enough to see it, you should take a photograph and place it in your home as it will bring peace of mind to all the family.

There are tales told of a lake monster that is known as 'Tessie' and is supposed to have inhabited Lake Tahoe in California, USA. Does it – or did it – exist?

There really was a creature that lived at the bottom of the lake. It had legs and could stay at the bottom of the lake for as long as it wanted. However, it did have to surface to eliminate its waste from its stomach, through its mouth, and then return to the bottom once again to continue feeding. It was not an intelligent creature and there were – or are – very few in existence. Perhaps only a few remain. The species has survived for many millions of years. In general shape, it is rather like a hippopotamus or an elephant.

It is a shy and timid creature, and would not seek out contact with human beings. We believe that there have been no sightings of the creature in recent years. Therefore, we are not sure if it still exists.

Did the 'Dover Demon,' a supposed bizarre creature that was seen in Boston, USA, really exist?

It did exist and was a crossbreed between two animals, an otter and a large rat. It had red albino eyes. Only three were born, with two dying at birth. The third one only lived for a short while. It could walk around on land, but it was much more at home in the water. Eventually, it was killed and eaten by other creatures.

What is the South American blood-sucking 'Chupacabra'?

This creature does exist and is similar in shape to a very small leopard. It is breeding and there are now quite a few around, but the numbers are kept low by the fact that they do not breed very often – only once every four years. They burrow underground, where they breed and live, and only come out at night.

They feed on animals and particularly domesticated farm animals that are easy prey for them, but they do not have to feed very often. They only suck the blood of the larger animals that they catch, but they also eat insects and other small creatures they find near their burrows.

It is a timid creature that does not want to be seen and is a crossbreed between a type of leopard and a wolf. They are not an ancient breed, but one that has developed in fairly recent times. Over time, they will develop further and start to also eat the meat of their prey rather than just drinking their blood.

What truth is there behind the 'Legend of the Dog-Man' from Michigan in the USA?

This was a story made up to cover the murder of a young girl. The murderer put the story of the wolf-like creature around to confuse others and to protect himself from detection. As he was from a wealthy background, the story was believed and he got away with the murder.

The Forbidden Plateau, in British Columbia, Canada, is where many people are alleged to have disappeared. Legend says that the plateau is inhabited by evil spirits. What is the truth of this mystery?

The Indian tribe that lived in the area, the Comox people, used the plateau as a safe hiding place for their women and children whenever they feared an attack from other tribes. There was such an attack and the women and children were sent up to the plateau as usual, but they were never seen again. The truth is that the women and children were captured, then all rounded up and taken away into some sort of slavery.

We have had it said to us by the spirits that lived at that time that although they were captive slaves, they lived a reasonable life in that they did not go hungry. None of them was killed at the place itself. There are no evil spirits on the plateau. That is just a legend. In fact, there are no human spirits there. The only spirits there now and that occupy the place are those of the animals that lived in the area.

Do you know anything about the Stone Spheres of Costa Rica at the Diquis Delta?

These spheres were made as an attempt to attract the gods. Each wealthy family had at least one set, the largest of them being for the head of the family. They believed that the spheres would protect them against evil spirits, and the land where they were kept was considered to be holy ground that attracted good spirits. When people died and were cremated, they often had their ashes scattered around the stone spheres as it was holy ground.

The stones were originally grouped into four circles and people would walk among them and pray there. It was – and still is – a very holy place. If you have an illness, you can go there, be touched by a spirit and possibly recover. People used to go there to get a cure for an illness by the touching of the stones, although the cure or improvement was rarely instantaneous. It wasn't a kind of on-the-spot miracle cure, but a sort of turning point towards better health that usually happened… and still does.

A lot of seemingly miraculous things have happened there, but they have never been written about. People also used to be taken there if they were about to die. You would have to have been a very wealthy and influential person to have had one of these stone spheres on your own land. Most people had to go to where the larger number of stones were kept and displayed.

This holy area must not be destroyed and it must be kept as it is today. It must be kept available for people to visit if they need to, not closed to the public like some similar ancient sites, for example Stonehenge. There are a lot of spirits that gather there, and also many ashes are scattered there.

The lines of Nazca are comprised of a widespread collection of huge patterns and representations of birds, spiders and so on drawn in the earth on

111

the coast of Peru probably over a thousand years ago. What is the explanation for them being there at all?

These are giant drawings of native animals such as tarantulas, monkeys, iguanas and condors that were marked into the ground by certain areas being cleared of stones and rocks, and other areas being left alone. It was believed by the primitive peoples who then lived there that the evil spirits were in the sky and flew around up above them. Therefore, it was thought that by carving giant spiders and other creatures, the evil spirits would be both frightened away and would stay away.

What is the truth about the starchild skulls found in 1930 in the mountains near Chihuahua in Mexico?

A very tall man had a brief sexual encounter with a female midget who had a very deformed face. He was twenty-seven years old and she was only eighteen. She became pregnant by him and had a son, whom she loved dearly, although he, too, had terrible facial deformities. The child did not live for very long and the mother died very, very soon after. They were buried together. They are now very happy in the spirit world and do not see the father.

Do you know anything about the sightings of 'The Loveland Frog' in 1952 and 1972 in Loveland, Ohio?

These animals did exist and were creatures that lived in the water. They emerged from the water and were able to stand, but not fully. They had feet like a frog, but were much larger in size. The majority of them lived in the water, but there were a few brave and curious ones who wanted to explore the land. This is the way God developed the animals through the natural evolution process. They are kind of leftovers from those times.

This was exactly the same way as other creatures progressed from the water to the land to breed. These creatures still exist, but in the water. The Loveland Frog story about creatures with glowing wands and sparks is nothing but a myth.

In 1969, a NASA scientist claimed that the sounds and vibrations recorded by the moon landing instruments meant that the moon was hollow. Is this possible?

The surface of the moon is in many ways similar to that of our planet earth and the moon is not hollow. If we were to dig below the surface of the moon, we would find vast mineral deposits including gold, diamonds, etc. The bell ringings and the tremors recorded occurred because heavier parts of the spacecraft crashed onto the surface of a canyon and just below it was a dried up underground lake bed. This caused such an intense echoing.

What is the truth about the mystery of Lake Michigan in the USA where a sailing ship, the Griffon, laden with furs, disappeared in 1679 on her maiden voyage?

Before the lake was formed, dinosaurs walked on these plains. There were also two mountains there, which are now completely submerged under the water. They are so very close together that they almost appear like one mountain. There is a gap in the shape like a sort of funnel. This funnel is about five miles wide at the top and about one mile wide just above seabed level.

On the seabed are very strong undercurrents that sometimes meet from opposite directions. Such an intense turbulence is created when they meet that water is violently pushed up the funnel to the surface of the sea rather like a geyser. It then collapses just as violently causing anything floating on it in that area to be sucked back down the funnel.

This explanation came from a sailor who was on the ship that disappeared when this happened. He says that he was thrown up in the air from the violent surge of water that suddenly came from below and went right up above the surface. The ship rose up, was turned over and everyone was sucked down through the funnel until they reached the seabed. They were then pulled across the seabed by the strong current and trapped under the shelf of the seabed floor.

The screaming tunnel. The so-called 'screaming tunnel' is located on the north-west side of Niagara Falls, near Ontario, Canada. The tunnel was originally built as part of the railway network being expanded by the Great Trunk Railroad Company. Although the company completed the construction of the long, cold and dark tunnel, it was overtaken by bankruptcy in the early 1900s and the railway track was never laid through the tunnel.

The story that surrounds the tunnel is that many years ago, a young girl trying to escape from a blazing farmhouse nearby ran into the tunnel in a pitiful attempt to extinguish her burning clothing. Her efforts were to no avail, the story tells, and she was engulfed in her own flaming funeral pyre.

They say that she screamed as her hair scorched away and that if you ever enter the tunnel and strike a match, her terrified screams can still be heard. Then, in a rush of wind, your match will immediately go out. Is this true?

Most of it is not true. When the tunnel was being built, it was a time when ruthless developers used child and adolescent labour as it was cheap and the youngsters were easy to exploit. A lot of the young people were between about fifteen and seventeen years old and were good labourers. They were mostly unskilled and used to carry rocks and stones out of the diggings.

They also had the jobs of fetching bread, water and fuel for the digging lamps used by the men working inside extending the tunnel. There were frequent injuries and rock falls, and on a number of occasions there were fires from badly maintained fuel stores and cooking fires.

About twenty children and youngsters were killed during the period when the tunnel was being dug. Many are still in the tunnel to this day, walking up and down in the darkness. They are not ghosts. They are young spirits who died there and stay there to play and be with spiritual friends who also died there. It is not possible for living people to see them, but they can sometimes be heard.

The story of the girl being burned in her clothing is not true. It was a girl being molested and mistreated, probably sexually as that was common in the dark tunnel where bad goings-on were not at all rare. The youngsters had no protection and were often victimised, sometimes very seriously in this way. The stories of the burning girl were made up. Not true.

The coldness of the stone and the atmosphere was due to where they dug the tunnel. It was – and is – very damp there, and there is a lot of water draining under the tunnel. That was why they never put the track down for trains. It wasn't safe and that's why they didn't carry on with the plan. If anyone lights a match there, what they hear is not ghosts screaming, but the shrieking of the large numbers of bats that live in the tunnel and are disturbed by the sudden light. No-one screams.

The headless ghost of Queen's Road in St John's, Newfoundland Province, Canada. The legend says that a tall, headless man in the dress of a sea captain was seen carrying a glowing light by a Mr Pettyham, who was returning home late one evening. When he was just outside his own house, the ghost appeared to him and Mr Pettyham ran inside in terror. Was this a real ghost?

Yes, it was. This ghost does exist, but he is not as tall as he is reputed to be. He is about 5ft 7 ins tall and he was not headless, but wore a hooded cloak. He was not a local ship's captain either, despite what the legend says. The whole reason for the sighting was that the ghost was helping the man to find his way to the house.

The ghost haunts the lane and the grounds of the house. Up the lane and near to the property was a small cottage where the ghost of this man and his family lived. His child died in the cottage and he is still looking for the spirit of the child who has gone to Heaven. This ghost has not gone to Heaven. The ghost is harmless to any human being.

Chapter 10

AMERICAN GHOSTS
Some Famous Ones Explained

The Ghost at Bachelor's Grove

Bachelor's Grove Cemetery is considered to be one of the most haunted cemeteries in America. It is located in Midlothian, Illinois. There have been numerous reports of many different, unexplained sightings of apparitions. There is even a photo taken in 1991 of a young woman from the past and dressed in white, sitting on a tombstone.

Is the cemetery really haunted and, if so, why by so many spirits? Why is this cemetery so important to the ghosts and is the photo real?

This is a very haunted cemetery indeed, and the reason for this is that there is a lot of energy coming up through the ground as a soft, golden light. The ground underneath it is full of spiritual energy, which can sometimes happen in various parts of the world. Spirits have always flocked there to these places as they find them very tranquil and happy. It is a very safe and peaceful place for spirits, and they congregate there because of that.

The picture is of the spirit of a woman who lost two children at birth. They are buried there in the cemetery and she often comes to visit their grave. They are also with her in the spirit world, but they, too, like to visit the graveyard.

[Note: At this point in the 'reading,' the actual spirit of the woman in the picture came to Wilf and explained everything about the cemetery. The next two paragraphs are written here in her own words.]

'My parents and other friends also come to visit the graveyard with me and my two children. It is also a favourite meeting place for many thousands of us spirits. There are many poor people like myself who could not afford a proper burial and many of us are buried here, sometimes in family graves. Anything to do with natural stone gives off energy and creates a natural and peacefully secure meeting place for spirits.

'I did not know that the photograph was being taken and I am pleased that people can see me. I hope that in this way people will realise that they do not ever really leave their loved ones. I am so pleased to come here to help answer these questions. I hope the world will be all right. The spirits are very concerned at the way in which the world has been mistreated. Please take care of our world and its special energy places. We do not want the cemetery or our meeting place, as we think of it, to be destroyed.'

The Haunted Railroad Crossing

Located south of San Antonio, Texas, there is an intersection between a road and the railway track. Several children were killed there in a tragic accident. It is said locally that on a number of occasions and by different people, the ghosts of the children have been spotted pushing cars across the track, even though the road is uphill. There is also a photo taken of what looks to be the ghost of a little girl with her dog. What is behind this story?

The answer is that the children that were killed there have not left the spot. They still play there. They are still children in the spirit world. So how do they manage to push a car across the track? They have been given extra-special energy by their ancestral spirits because it is where they died. These other spirits also help if a car needs pushing off the track for safety reasons. As it is the place where their spirits lost their earthly lives, left their bodies and went to Heaven, they all want the area to be kept clear for them to play.

They are sad for their families that they have left behind. Many of their families have now joined them. This will continue for many centuries yet.

The Bell Witch

This legend started as long ago as 1817 in Tennessee. Supposedly, there was a house there that was haunted by a witch called Kate Batts. The Bell family, who lived in the house at that time, claimed they were kicked and scratched, that their hair was pulled, blankets were taken off the beds and strange sounds were heard. These included unknown voices and cries, and usually happened on a regular daily basis and when the witch's form also frequently appears. What should we think of this tale?

There is also a John Bell connected with the legend. He was not a very nice person. He was cruel and was known to have forced himself sexually onto a number of the female slaves and domestic workers on his estate. The vengeance sought by Kate Batts against him was because of what he did to young girls, including the daughter of a very close friend, among many others. These events generally happened in his bedroom and he even locked girls in there overnight.

Kate Batts was not a witch, but merely a woman who cared about the young women that he had raped and even murdered. This fact is not mentioned in the legend. She has never let John Bell rest in the spirit world and she continues to move him on from place to place, so that he cannot be with his loved ones. Kate does this as his punishment for what he did to others. He is always running away from her, but can never be free of her.

Kate was trying to let everyone know what had happened to her daughter's friend and other young women and also to protect others from John Bell. His death was celebrated in the spirit world due to the cruelty that he had inflicted on others during his lifetime. He cannot be punished in the spirit world, but he can be shamed and they can make his life difficult there.

In the most part, this is a true story except that Kate Batts was not a witch, just a woman who both cared about others. She knew the truth about John Bell and sought revenge. There are no such beings as witches.

The Amherst Poltergeist

This happened in 1878 in Amherst, North Central Nova Scotia, New Brunswick, Canada. A young girl lived with her married sister. She was physically attacked and molested by a man called Bob MacNeal.

Soon after that, she apparently became open to violent attacks from time to time by totally unseen entities. The women also claimed to see something moving under the covers in their beds at night. One of the girls was choking and struggling for breath. Her body was heating up, her skin was stretching and her eyes were bulging out of her head. Very loud noises were emanating from under the bed. What was the reason for this terrifying ordeal?

The two young women in this legend were being protected by a friendly spirit from a man who was trying to harm them. The man was deeply obsessed with the young girl, who was called Esther, and also with her sister. He was intent upon harming and he may well have injured one or both of them but for the intervention of the spirit, who was trying to protect them rather than cause harm to the girls.

The spirit that protected the young women has told us that she was eventually killed by this man and that the man buried her close by and near to a waterfall. Her method of protection was to cause upheavals and disturbance, and to divert the harmful situation away from the young girls. As a punishment for his wickedness, his spirit is forced to wander in heaven and is not allowed to settle down.

Chapter 11

MYSTERIES, MYTHS AND LEGENDS
FROM ELSEWHERE

What is the 'Eltanin Antenna' that was discovered and photographed in the Antarctic Ocean in 1964 and is reputed to be a living or previously living creature?

It isn't and was never alive. It is mechanical. A ship sank in a freak storm and is buried in soft silt below the antenna. The mast of the ship had an antenna attached. There is gold and silver bullion in the holds of that early merchant ship. The ship was on an illegal smuggling run. It was not properly registered and its loss was never totally documented. The antenna seen is actually the top part of the buried mast of the vessel.

Boadicea

Boudicca, as she was then known, was queen of the British tribe, the Iceni, in the region of Eastern England [now Suffolk and Norfolk] and Kent in the middle years of the 1st century AD.

Under the Romans who had recently invaded, her husband, King Prasutagus, was ruler, but when he died, leaving Boadicea a widow, the Roman

invaders decided to take over and rule in his place.
The tribal lands and wealth were all seized. This
act and the cruelty used incensed Boadicea, who
then led a revolt against Roman rule. What really
happened?

There was more to it than just the Romans taking
over. In addition to that, they deliberately humiliated
the Briton noble families and mistreated their
womenfolk. There were several pitched battles in
the revolt. There is a legend that many thousands of
Roman soldiers died, but this is nonsense.

There were only a few thousand Romans in the
entire country at that time, so the battles were not
the sort of massive battles that we heard of in later
campaigns. Only about fifty to a hundred men took
part on each side on the first two occasions. There
was no heavy weaponry used; the battles were
fought with swords and spears only.

The first battle took place at Colchester and was
fiercely contested with great carnage and cruelty on
both sides. It lasted for over four hours and almost
everyone that took part in it was either killed or
wounded. Afterwards, Boadicea burned down the
town of Colchester and also part of the outskirts of
London, including its busy market. She also attacked
the stronghold of the Roman legion and put to the
sword as many soldiers as could be found.

The Romans retaliated and there was finally a
big battle fought, also near Colchester, at which the
tribesmen were defeated once and for all. It is not
true, as some say, that Boadicea took poison rather
then let herself be captured and tormented by the
victors. She was actually in the middle of the pitched
battle actively taking part when she was surrounded,

overcome and run through the stomach at sword point. The nearby Romans, seeing she was down, then fell upon her and repeatedly stabbed her even after she was dead.

They also captured Boadicea's daughters, who had been bravely fighting alongside their warrior mother. They stripped and humiliated them, whipped them and mutilated them repeatedly until and even after they were dead. Their bodies and that of the butchered queen were paraded around for everyone to see and learn the dangers of rebellion against Roman rule. That's the true story.

Lady Godiva

Lady Godiva, wife of the Anglo-Saxon Earl Leofric of Mercia, is said to have lived in the middle of the 11th century. She is most famous for the story that she rode on horseback through the streets of the Coventry city entirely naked.

Legend has it that she did this in response to a bet to make her husband reduce the city's heavy tax burden. Did this event really happen and, if so, why?

It did happen, but not quite the way the story tells. Lady Godiva was a very wealthy member of the Saxon nobility that ruled in Britain before the Norman invasion. She was brought up by her mother very strictly. She was a very religious woman and a devoted follower of Jesus Christ. She was well-liked and well-respected.

Nevertheless, she had several affairs with men before she decided that she truly wanted to be with Leofric. There was friction developing between the earl and the other nobleman with whom she had her last affair. A duel was fought and her ex-lover was killed.

Feeling that she was partly responsible and that she had sinned, Godiva sought to punish herself before her God and although she had never been on a horse before, she chose to ride naked and in shame and humiliation before the people. This, she felt, would help cleanse her of her misdeeds and her sins. She also thought the act of remorse would restore her virginity as well as her self-respect.

The story got out about what she was going to do. As she was very well thought of in the city, it turned out that when she rode through the streets, all the people of the place stayed indoors until she had passed. As a result, although she was covered by her hair being draped around her body, there was no-one there to see after all.

She was not Leofric's wife when she made the ride, but married him later. She had two children by him, both of them girls. There is no truth in the legend that her ride was an effort by her to help the poor people and their taxation. That is all a bit how the story got mixed up. Her ride was just a sort of confessional and an attempt at deliberate retribution for her sorrow at her past deeds. However, when Leofric learned of the friendly respect shown by the people, he did free the people from their taxes and tolls. History has connected the stories and, as so often, got them a bit confused.

Jason and the Golden Fleece

The story of Jason and his Argonauts has been told in one form or another for some three thousand years yet no-one knows whether it is truth or legend. They say he was born of the great family of Greek gods, that he was dispossessed and, after years of searching with his sailors, found the Golden Fleece and was thus restored to his lands and his status. Is there any truth in this story?

Yes, there is, but not an awful lot. That's the way with so many legends and folk stories. There really was such a person as Jason and he was the true-born son of the king of a region in ancient Greece.

The idea that he was a child of the gods is nonsense as there were no such things as gods. The truth of the matter is that Jason's father was rather a weak and unpopular king and his brother, Jason's uncle, tried to steal the throne from Jason's father. When he did, Jason was banished for many years on pain of death. He had no way to support himself so gathered a group of mercenaries and sailors and set off to make his fortune in any way he could – robbery, pillage, theft and piracy.

It's not true that they went on any particular quest for any particular thing. They were just out for what they could get. He and his men were later said to have sailed in a boat called the Argo, but no-one here has ever heard of that. Over the years they had a number of different boats.

Anyway, after several years, they arrived by pure chance at a place in what is now Turkey and found the local people were panning the streams for gold washed down from the hills. They had invented their own method of filtering large volumes of the river waters that carried the gold dust by straining it through a number of sheep and goat-skins.

Sometimes the sheep-skins could contain considerable deposits of gold dust. The skins were then hung up to dry so that the precious dust could be gently shaken from them. These gold-laden sheepskins were what became known as the Golden Fleece, but there wasn't just one of them. There were lots.

Jason and his men robbed the people and stole many fleeces and other supplies of gold. With the new riches, he was able to go back to his home, raise a larger group of helpers and reclaim his rights to become king.

Queen Hatshepsut

The only recorded 'great' female pharaoh was Queen Hatshepsut, who reigned over all Egypt from 1472-58 BC. She was known to have been a prolific builder and a powerful sovereign yet after her death, many of her monuments and statues were pulled down and destroyed. In other places, her likeness was deliberately defaced or had other resemblances superimposed on them. Was this the work of her stepson Thutmose?

Yes, it was. Although she was married to Thutmose II, who did not live very long, Thutmose III was his son, but not hers. Thutmose III was a capable general and very greedy for power and wealth. When his father died, the queen acted for a while as a regent for the young next pharaoh, but after a while, she took over everything for herself and even wore men's clothing and a false beard like the real male pharaohs.

The young prince was also jealous of Hatshepsut and when she had daughters of her own, he was concerned that she might make one of them pharaoh instead of himself. He was secretly her enemy all the time, even when he was leading her armies to victories.

Hatshepsut lost one of her little daughters who was stillborn and she had her buried behind a massive wall in one of her temples. The baby was adorned with much gold and silver and jewels. Thutmose had learned about this and thought he would add that wealth to his own. In fact, he failed to find the girl's tomb. No-one has found it to this day. It is undiscovered and is still there perfectly intact with the girl's mummy and the fabulous tomb items with which she was buried still safely hidden from men's eyes.

Not many people have realised it, but Queen Hatshepsut died as a result of being poisoned on the orders of her stepson. She did not just die naturally; she was murdered. When she was gone, all her wealth was immediately confiscated by members of her family and Thutmose found he had much less than he thought. He was very angry at what had happened. He seized total power and went on to lead Egypt to one of the greatest periods of its history.

There were two reasons why her buildings and palaces and statues were destroyed and defaced. First was that all along he knew she had buried the baby with all that wealth and he had many of his men searching for it. As part of the search, they pulled down and smashed many of the statues as well as wrecking lots of the queen's buildings. It was plain desperation and greed.

The other reason was that the Egyptian royals believed their success in passing on to their new life after death was through the messages sent by their sacred statues and impressive temples. Destroying those would, it was thought, mean that the memory of the dead queen would fade and that wherever she was, revenge was working on her as she would not be able to become immortal.

Tutankhaten, also known as Tutankhamen

Tutankhamen was a young Egyptian king [pharaoh] who reigned over Upper and Lower Egypt from 1336-1327 BC. In his early years, he was known as Tutankhaten as the father, [Amenhotep IV, also known as Akhenaton] of his brother, the previous pharaoh, had started a new religion. On his brother's death, he came to the throne at the age of seventeen as he was already married to one of Akhenaton's daughters.

Tutankhamen died mysteriously while still a youngster. Although his tomb was discovered in 1922, there remain doubts about how he met his death. What was the cause?

The boy king was only a ruler theoretically. Even when he reached his teens, he had very little to do with running the country. He was mostly a symbolic king and never made any important decisions. All the real governing was done by his senior officers, priests and ministers, especially his family relatives and the general in charge of the Egyptian armies.

Before he died, they had all been instructed by the boy's father that they were to look after him. They had sworn to do this and kept their promises in the beginning.

Like his father before him, he had trouble with his legs and feet. He could never walk very well and was therefore very under-confident. He kept himself to himself and used to keep away from others if and when he could. He was an intelligent boy when he got older, but to start with, he appeared to people to be rather simple and never really knowing what he was doing or what he was saying. He was well protected and cared for, and knew that he could give orders or say things that would be done.

He first became seriously ill when he was fifteen, but after a while he recovered. Then when he was about seventeen, he became ill again. The people who had assumed power realised by now that he was a physical liability as a king and that this might get worse if he got used to power as he grew older. This they thought could be bad for Egypt. They were therefore determined to get rid of him and laid plans in readiness. When he fell ill the second time, he was quickly poisoned.

The poison did not kill him outright, but it weakened him. He had a serious fall from his chariot and broke his leg. He died a few days later. His death was not announced at once because he was having a lot of building done and his ministers felt this should be completed first to avoid any suspicions.

Most members of the royal family at that time had their wealth and possessions taken away from them and given to the men who took over. They took everything he had except for his personal jewellery and treasures. These were buried with him and were later moved with his mummy when his original tomb was taken over by his successor for his own use. His own funeral things were sacred and although they were valuable, to steal them could bring bad luck on the thieves. That's why all his things remained to be discovered less than a hundred years ago.

Tutankhamen never grew up. He never really had a chance. He now sits in the spirit world and travels only to be with his famous death mask whenever that is taken somewhere. Wherever it goes, he goes. He is made very happy that he can always see the mask and also by the fact that everywhere people want to see him and read about him.

Will we ever find the Holy Grail?

Of course not. It was supposed to be the goblet that Jesus drank from at the Last Supper. As there never was a Last Supper, the Holy Grail does not exist and never has existed. It is all just a myth that has carried on over the years.

Who made the Turin Shroud?

The real shroud that Jesus was buried in was a length of cloth that was wrapped around his body soon after he died. Its remains are still in his as yet undiscovered tomb with him. Several people drew pictures of Jesus during his lifetime and one particular picture was done shortly before his death. About five or six of these drawings are still hidden in Jerusalem. The Turin Shroud is a fake. It has nothing whatsoever to do with Jesus.

Several great kings and rulers in history have owned what they believed was the Sword of Destiny, the name given to the Holy Lance that was used to pierce Jesus' side. In recent centuries it has become lost. What really happened to it?

This did not exist as such. This weapon was one of those used by the Roman soldiers on Jesus and the robbers that he died alongside mostly to torment and goad them. None of them was killed in this way and this sword did not cause Jesus to die. The Romans slit their wrists and ordered the people and their soldiers to stone Jesus and the robbers. It was this that caused their deaths.

Jesus was crucified on a cross, but it remained on the ground, and this is how he died – by stoning.

Crucified, laid on the ground and facing the sun, then stoned to death. His side was never pierced and the Biblical story about that is all legend.

What is the Sphinx? It is claimed that the Sphinx was built 4,000 years ago about the same time as the three largest pyramids. What was the reason for its construction?

The Sphinx is just a statue of a lion with the head and face of a pharaoh. It has, and never has had, any other significance or power.

The pyramids in Cairo in Egypt were built about 4,500 years ago. Why were they built in the way they were?

The kings and pharaohs of that time believed in evil spirits and feared that they would enter the pyramids and cause sacrilege. Therefore, the pyramids were built in that particular shape because they believed that the evil spirits would not be able to grip or hold on to the sides of the pyramids and therefore would not be able to enter the tombs and defile the corpses of those buried there. Therefore, the pyramids were built as a protection for the dead.

How were these massive pyramids built by such primitive people?

To start with, although primitive by today's standards, these people of Ancient Egypt were very knowledgeable and very skilled in many ways. Contrary to popular belief, the pyramids were not built in an upward direction, but built downward from the existing desert floor into a giant hole previously dug in preparation. The hole was boarded around the sides and then water was poured in to create a flat surface for marking levels. The massive stones were then lashed together, rather like the rungs of a rope ladder. These were laid out on the surface and added to gradually as each was lowered over the edge.

The stones that remained on the surface acted as counterweights and were pushed forward inch by inch on log rollers. When the stones reached their level, they were lowered onto log rollers and then rolled into position. The stones were always lowered into position and never lifted as it has been believed over the years. This was the simplest way for the pyramid to be constructed at the time it was built. Once the bottom level was in position, the support boarding was moved inwards and doubled as a platform for the men to work from. Then the gap was back-filled with sand. The whole process then began again with the next layer.

So the stones were not raised at all, but lowered into place. When the construction was complete, the surrounding area was cleared down to the existing bedrock level where it stands today.

Why does the Great Pyramid of Giza not have a top stone as have the others?

The top stones were left off until the burial of a particular pharaoh, but this never happened. This was because the pharaoh that should have occupied the pyramid died of a disease, and in such circumstances, the body was cremated then buried elsewhere in a very deep grave.

In those days, they believed that if someone died of a disease rather than of natural causes or died in battle, they would not rest in a pyramid or return to the Underworld in a proper manner. Consequently, at Giza the last stones, the symbolic top of the pyramid, were never put into place.

Who were really buried in the mastaba, the numerous Egyptian tombs?

There are some kings, queens and pharaohs in these tombs. However, many of them were used just for very wealthy people. These people had the tombs built for them before their deaths, and their gold and precious stones were buried with them. The Egyptians believed at that time that with a tomb of rock and stone around them, both spirit and their wealth would be safe for all time.

All too many were afraid that they would not get into Heaven because of the bad things that they did in their lifetime. They hoped that they would be able to buy their way into the spirit world by pleasing the gods with their gold and jewels. They did not foresee that people coming later would be different and would not have the same beliefs. As a result, these later people broke open the tombs, threw out the mummies and took the treasures for themselves.

The Loch Ness Monster. Does it – or did it – ever exist?

It never existed as such, but there were several very large fish-like creatures with fan tails that lived deep in the loch. They were very long fish and only came to the surface when they were very sick or dying.

When they appeared on the surface of the loch in their sick or dying state, they curled their body around, so that it appeared that they had humps and they looked almost like dragons. They would try to return to deep water, but would be eaten by other fish or their own kind. That is why they have never found any trace of these creatures and we do not believe there are any left. Please remember we cannot enter water to find out.

The lost island of Atlantis. Did it exist, and if so, where is its location?

Yes, the island did exist, but they built the city in the wrong place. The land belonged to the sea. The land rose out of the sea through an underground volcanic eruption and was supported purely by the gases underneath.

The soil was soft. They built a city with massive imported granite stones and the second volcanic eruption from underneath the soil burst upwards releasing the gases supporting Atlantis. Once this pressure was released, the land returned down to its original level under the sea, taking the city of Atlantis down with it.

The location of Atlantis is on the south-west coast of India near to the Republic of Goa and is over thirty miles offshore. The sea in that area is still warm from the continuous volcanic eruptions that occur on the seabed. There are still the remains of buildings resting on the ledge of the cliff, next to where the city was submerged.

Does or did the Yeti, or the Abominable Snowman as he is also known, ever exist?

No. The yeti was just a very big bear-like animal often covered in snow that lived in that area and was searching for food.

Do – or did – dragons ever exist?

Yes, but they did not breathe fire or fly. They were just examples of a large now extinct reptile.

Although firmly embedded in Scandinavian folklore, the lake monster of Lake Storsdon in Storsjoodjuret, NW Jamtland, Sweden was last seen in the early 17th century. What was it and does it still exist?

This creature existed in diminishing numbers until a few hundred years ago. It has not been seen since that time. This creature had legs and humps, and could walk under water. This information came from spirits that lived at that time and they believe that the creatures lived around the shores of the lake rather than under the water. They fed on plankton and grass, and were sometimes seen going across the lake. They were too big and clumsy to breed well and were also prey for other animals.

What is the truth about the fairy spirit that wails to warn of impending death in Irish legend known as the banshee?

This is nothing more than a legend from a country of people with vivid imaginations. In years gone by in Ireland, many people feared death and they would pray and hope that an angel would come and take them to heaven. The legend of the banshee is a story that has been passed down through many generations of Irish families, along with that of fairies and leprechauns, which are also nothing more than fantasy.

What was the succubus seen in medieval theological illustrations? And did it really exist?

This was a true story and the one and only original succubus was the spirit of a beautiful young woman. Unfortunately, she was deformed from the waist to her chest area, so she never had a sexual relationship and passed over at the age of thirty-three years.

She was a very intelligent and caring person, and would often try to come back to try and make love to men in her ghostly form. After many unsuccessful attempts to do this, she decided to go to heaven and now she is at peace.

It was a bone disease that crippled her. Unfortunately, her brother, who was known as the incubus, also suffered from the same bone condition. He died after his sister and had the same problem with sexual relationships in his lifetime. He, too, tried to make love to women in his ghostly form, but was unsuccessful. The idea that there were lots of these creatures floating about ready to molest people in their sleep is utter nonsense.

What is the 'Mongolian death worm' that is alleged to exist in the Ghobi Desert?

This creature does not exist and was dreamt up by someone who wanted to frighten people away from a certain area of the desert for their own reasons.

Does the flesh-eating creature of Filipino legend known as the 'Aswang' really exist or has ever existed?

This is just a story that has been handed down through families and generations. It never existed.

Do mermaids exist?

There were mermaids of a sort that evolved, but they had a face similar to that of a monkey. They were not yet human in appearance. God's heavenly spirits realised that it was not the direction they wanted to go towards producing His spiritual children. Therefore, this creature was not allowed to breed and eventually died out.

Can you explain the legend of the 'White cavalry' that was alleged to have appeared in 1918 to the troops in the trenches in France?

There was no white cavalry. It was all made up. The occasion that gave rise to it happened on a rather dull and misty day when the low sun of the late afternoon broke through the cloud and came through shining very brightly across no-man's-land. The sun shone straight into the eyes of the German troops in their trenches and the blinding light played tricks on their eyes and minds.

There had also been a prolonged shortage of food, clean water and warm clothing. The constant deprivation, endless danger and death of their compatriots had affected the troops' morale very badly. The troops had also been isolated from the main German army contingents and therefore felt very vulnerable and alone. The German line was being held by young teenage boys and elderly men who were neither well trained nor used to battle conditions. They were a sort of Dad's Army. They were just frightened men and boys.

All of these things, combined with the constant noise of bullets being fired, continuous bombardment from exploding shells and scattered reflections caused by the sun from weapons and equipment created odd shadows and apparitions. These were something like the mirages or hallucinations as you would imagine are seen in the desert. These hallucinations confused the Germans.

It is not surprising that under such wretched and dangerous conditions, one of the men thought he saw something magical. He called out to the others that he could see a huge battalion of ghost riders charging them cavalry-like through the clouds and across the devastated land in front of the trenches. The soldier asked his comrades if they could see it too. Others were then immediately sure they could also see it. Some started to cry or pray while others ran away, starting a panic in the ranks.

Later, the whole story was told many times over and became more and more exaggerated. In fact, it was really mostly the result of a lot of men and boys who concocted the story for fear of repercussions and being labelled as cowards for running from the battle.

What was the Angel of Mons?

This was supposed to have appeared in August 1914 at the beginning of the First World War. The truth is that it never happened at all. This myth originates from a short story written by a famous Welsh author of the day. For some reason, over time it became regarded as a true story, which it was not. There was never an Angel of Mons.

The Bermuda Triangle in the Atlantic Ocean, or 'The Devil's triangle,' as some have called it, is where ships and aircraft have disappeared mysteriously.

What is the truth of this widely held belief?

The Bermuda Triangle is located over one of the deepest parts of that area of ocean. There is a shelf over one mile below the surface of the ocean. The shelf has a hole near its centre and this hole is over twenty miles in diameter. Three to five times a year, spasmodic volcanic eruptions may occur on the seabed.

These, heating the water to high temperatures, naturally cause the water to rise. This in turn draws more water from the seabed and the hot water passes up through the gap in the shelf to reach the surface. When it cools, it collapses again suddenly. This, in effect, causes an underwater 'waterfall' around the edge of the shelf. This violently sucks water and air down from the surface like a funnel. Anything that is in that area at the time, such as boats, low-flying planes, etc, can easily get sucked down too. Stay away from this area.

The White Horse of Uffington is a carving of a horse in the turf of an English hillside. It measures some 110 metres long. What is the relevance of the image and why is it so big?

This picture of a horse carved out of the hillside was done very many years ago. It was a design that was supposed to frighten off flying evil spirits and to stop them from killing the domestic animals in the area. It is man-made and was cut out in a very clever way. It is a spiritual thing and there should be an old village nearby which has been buried under the ground. This could be of great interest to both historians and archaeologists.

How did they transport the giant foundation stones to form the base for the Temple of Jupiter at Baalbek in Lebanon?

It was easier than it looks. A giant canal was built that ran the couple of miles from the quarry where the stones were located to the site of the temple. This canal was designed to transport all the heavy rocks. The men who built the temple cut the rocks in such a way on the underside that they appeared to be supported by four legs, rather like a table.

A wooden raft was then constructed underneath the stone to support it. The 'legs' were then chipped away and the massive stone descended onto the raft. The canal was then flooded with water and the stone on the raft was floated to the site of the temple. After the temple was completed, the canal that had been created to enable the movement of stones was filled in and covered over once again.

Ancient wooden bird model

There was an object found at Saqquara in Egypt in 1898 which is reputed to have been created in approximately 200 BC. It is on show in the centre hall of the Cairo Museum and has been labelled as a model aeroplane. For an object over 2,200 years old, this appears to be quite an achievement.

Experts feel that it has the correct proportions to qualify to be a push glider. The Egyptians were also known to make scale models of projects they planned later to create or build. What exactly is this strange object?

It belonged to a very wealthy man who believed that when he died, his spirit would go into the wooden bird and that he would fly up to Heaven to be with the gods.

It may look like an aeroplane, but he did not know anything of aeroplanes back in those times. He just designed a bird that neither got off of the ground nor went anywhere. He did not think that it would really fly, but he thought that his spirit would go into it and then fly to Heaven in a symbolic way. His treasure is still buried in the tomb where they found the bird. It is buried underneath the floor.

What is the true story of the ship, the Mary Celeste, found drifting and abandoned in 1872?

There was a very important man on board and his enemies secretly poisoned the ship's provisions. This caused hallucinations, sent the people crazy and caused them to throw themselves into the water and to drown. The last person left on the ship set the sails before jumping off.

The reason for the ship being so far away from land and off course at the time when it was found was the changing winds and the fact that it had been adrift without people on board for more than ten days.

What happened to another vessel, the yacht, the Marie Celeste that disappeared on 20th April, 2007?

The crew of three was on deck during a period of very rough weather. A freak wave washed them all overboard. That is all that happened.

What was the original reason for the building of Stonehenge in about 3,500-1,100 BC?

The stones originally came from Wales in Great

Britain and were brought to Wiltshire in England by river in the first instance and then overland by ox cart or by rolling on logs. These stones were very large and carefully selected, and the stones that were taken were the largest that were transportable.

The original idea was to build a temple or other holy building for ten-fifteen people, but the structure was also intended for the sick and dying. At that time, it was believed that you should die in the open air and that you would die faster. If you died indoors, they thought, evil spirits would stay in you and those that did could then pass on to other living humans.

When the stones reached Salisbury Plain, they were unloaded, but before they could start the construction work, the men building the structure were attacked. Some were killed, some fled and the women were carried off. They had been a peaceful and wealthy community and had no real means of protecting themselves. After the attack, the stones were left just lying there for about a thousand years or more.

At the time when the stones were put to use again, it was as a burial ground. The stones were stood on end to create a through draught around the ceremonial and burial fires. It was quite easy to stand them up using earth ramps. People were burned there after death and others also went there to pray.

Is the Antikythera mechanism as discovered in 1901 on the Greek island of the same name and reputed to be approximately 2,000 years old an ancient Greek computer?

Not exactly. Really, it was a clock-like mechanism that was originally thought could have been used to calculate the motions of the stars and planets. That

143

was not so. Really, it was just a navigation device which was placed on the front of a ship. It was designed by two people, one from Israel and the other from Crete in the Greek islands, and took two years to design and build.

The design was based on the principle of the spinning wheel and the spinning top, and when they played around with these ideas, they realised that they stopped at different places. They moved on to designing a device to navigate a ship, which spun around and tracked the course the ship was on. It was quite a successful device, but unfortunately, the ship sank in a very bad storm. To this day, there is a large amount of treasure still on the sunken ship.

The device's creators designed it because they wanted to travel the world more safely than was then possible. Although it was very crude and clumsy, it was a good invention for its time and was very similar to the first compass.

What is the Phaistos disc found in Crete (origin 1,700 BC) and why can it not be deciphered?

This is just a family tree that recorded the names of those born in that particular family through time. Some of the signs are the same, and this is just where the same or similar family names have been repeated through the generations.

What was the 2,000-year-old Baghdad battery used for?

This was a small vase discovered by workmen in 1936 that contained a copper cylinder and an iron rod. This was not a battery as was thought, but an invention created to check the clearness or quality of the water when testing new water holes. They used to dig a well, take a sample, place it in the vase and add a substance to the water to test how pure it was. The results of this testing procedure concluded which minerals were present in the water.

It was a crude device and there was little knowledge of the full range of minerals that might be present at that time. However, they tried to detect mainly for iron and tin. Again it was a clever device for its time, and it was also used as a test to determine whether the water found was pure and safe enough for drinking. It was also considered an indicator for whether it was worthwhile mining for iron and tin in that area.

Were the Dendera lamps a form of electric light for the Temple of Hathor in Iraq?

This was a very primitive generator that was based on friction and a revolving mechanism that was hand operated. Its basis was the rubbing of two metals together, one being iron with cane being used as insulation. It was not a strong light, more of a glow, and was used just to impress important dignitaries when they came to visit the temple.

The temple being a very important holy place, it was considered essential that it was kept exceptionally clean so they used young girls for the sweeping and cleaning of it at all times. This is the reason there were no traces of soot found when it was discovered.

Why was it impossible to decipher the Voynich manuscript, which is claimed to have been written in the fifteenth century?

A wealthy family had a baby daughter who was very

sick and who was what we would nowadays describe as both mentally and physically handicapped. Such children were usually done away with at birth in those days, but her parents loved her so much at her birth they just could not bear the thought of letting her go.

They knew that if they decided to keep her, they must hide her away secretly to protect her from others who, because of her state, might wish to kill her. To keep her occupied, her parents created the manuscript. Basically, it was a language that was made up by them and purely used as a secret language to communicate with the child, so it was only understood by the parents and her.

The manuscript or book was a collection written by her over many years and contained her writings, poems, recipes, etc. There was even a section showing the directions to Heaven for her when she died to prevent her from losing her way.

The parents thought that they could also use the manuscript to locate her spirit when they, too, eventually went to Heaven. The daughter died at the age of nineteen years.

What is the mystery of the 'Plain of Jars,' large stone jars found in Northern Laos in Asia?

These are burial urns. They were made on the site and their size was determined by either the size of the family or their wealth. The top of the jar was purposely left open to let the light in and the recently dead bodies were placed in them until they decomposed. So essentially they are a form of burial chambers.

The jars are very religious and spiritual vessels,

and they should not be tampered with. They should be left alone and, as a sign of respect, nothing else should now be put into them.

Were the photographs of the Cottingley Fairies all genuine?

They were genuine photographs, but they were not of genuine fairies. There is no such thing as a fairy. Some mischievous girls had taken photographs of dragonflies and butterflies, and these pictures were then manipulated to make the images appear to be fairies. Fairies are nothing but a harmless myth for a child's imagination.

Do you know anything about John Titor, the man who claimed to be a time traveller from the year 2036?

This man was a very clever and well-rehearsed trickster, who had a problem with a part of his brain, but was not a lunatic. He believed that he could con people for his own personal financial gain and had very intricate plans to do so.

The tale that he eventually disappeared back to his own time is nonsense. There is no such thing as time travel. He did not disappear at all. He just went back to his normal job and to his former life.

Who was the man they named the 'Nuremberg Enigma,' Kaspar Hauser, who appeared in the town square in 1828 and is believed to have been kept in captivity until the age of sixteen years?

He was born on a ship and kept in and taught to read and write by his mother. Kaspar was very intelligent and the reason he was not allowed out or to live a normal life was because of his wealthy father. His father wanted to keep it a secret that he had had an affair with a servant and felt so ashamed when she bore his child. So Kaspar was kept a prisoner and hidden away. The mother never married and lived as a servant to the father and two other families.

Kaspar was continuously kept a complete secret from the world because he bore a strikingly similar resemblance to his father and the father was still frightened of being found out. His mother grew tired of seeing her son cooped up and decided to help him escape.

This is not really a mystery as his mother wrote the letters to a local captain asking that he be allowed to join the cavalry and follow in his father's footsteps. The letters were written in such a way that if the father should get hold of them, he would think that they had come from someone else other than the mother. The real reason and sadness for the secrecy was that Kaspar's father was obviously a very well-known man and his mother was just a very lowly servant woman.

The boy had been, until then, locked up in a small shed-like structure and was looked after by his mother until she sent him on his way with the letters. His mother made sure that she went far away so that the boy's father could not find them. The reason that the boy was found wearing good quality but very old and worn clothing was to ensure that the boy would not be easily recognised.

What happened to the Derby-winning racehorse Shergar that was stolen from his trainer's stables in Ireland in 1983?

Shergar was stolen and transferred to a barn less than twenty miles away. The thieves hoped to get a really good ransom payment for him. The horse was locked in a hay barn, which he did not like as he wanted to be outside. He hated being locked in. Therefore, he made a lot of noise, kicking and whinnying; this frightened the thieves a great deal.

All the noise attracted attention from the immediate neighbours, which panicked the thieves so much that they shot Shergar only four days after stealing him. They then quickly buried him in a shallow pit underneath the barn floor.

The barn is still used for stacking hay to this day. One of the thieves was renting part of the land at the time of the theft. They did not really want to kill the horse, but their big mistake was to lock him in and cause him to panic.

Chapter 12

GHOSTS AND HAUNTED PLACES

The 'Phantom drummer of Tidworth.' This famous 'ghost' was reported in a house that once stood where Zouch Manor in Wiltshire, England now stands. According to early records, some said at the time that it was a harmful poltergeist which was able to cause a strange drumming sound and that he could do this while walking around over the roof. Is there any explanation for this?

There was a ghost haunting the property as he did not wish to go to Heaven straight away. He is still there. About three hundred years ago, there was a priest living in the house. He knew about the ghost and said he had seen him several times. He was holding services and performing rituals in an attempt to exorcise the ghost.

At roughly the same time, two young girls were staying at the house and slept in the bedroom that had belonged to the ghost in his lifetime. The ghost was angry that they were there and sleeping on his bed, so he banged on the inside of the cupboard in the room to frighten them away. There were no actual drums as such.

The ghost is that of a man aged about forty, and he had previously worked in the cellar of the house. He worked in the house for about fifteen years and died very suddenly from a heart disease. To this day he likes to stay in the house and sleep in that particular bedroom. He means no ill-will and is harmless.

The same house is also visited by the spirit of a huge dog that once lived there. He also moves freely about elsewhere in the village and has been seen in many places. A story has grown up that anyone who sees him will swiftly die. This is nonsense. He looks ferocious, but is in no way to be feared.

The Headless Drummer Boy, Dover Castle, England

The story goes that the headless drummer boy of Dover is the ghost of a fifteen-year-old lad, one Sean Flynn, who is quite frequently seen walking along the battlements late at night beating his drum. Locals believe he was decapitated by soldiers who thought he might be carrying a secret hoard of money for one of the high-ranking officers in the garrison.

There was a BBC attempt to exorcise the boy's ghost a year or so ago. Did it work and how much truth is there in the legend?

When they tried to exorcise the boy, it did not work properly. He is still there. It's true that the boy was murdered, but it was not for money. It was jealousy and because of the antics he got up to with some of the castle staff, especially female. He was a kind and considerate lad, but for his age, he was a serious woman's man and liked to have plenty of female company around. Many of the women found him more attractive than the other soldiers.

He did have money on him when he died, but it was not much and it was all returned. The fact is that the soldiers were drunk at the time. They waylaid him when he was going into town and when he was injured, they were afraid he would talk. So his head was cut off in sheer cold blood. So there is some truth in that part.

There is truth, too, in the belief that the boy does still haunt the castle. What is more, he does so along with two other people... a maid and a cook. The cook died when she was fifty and she haunts the lower reaches of the castle. The maid was a young lady who died of a brain tumour. She had had an affair with the drummer boy, as had plenty of others. They now wander through the castle and its grounds and they go up onto the battlements where he used to beat his drum for regimental calls and orders. They are usually hand-in-hand as they walk and that's often how people see them.

It was winter when the boy was killed and even now, as they walk, they stamp their feet to keep warm. That is what people sometimes hear. It is not actually a drum. During the day, they go down to the kitchen areas and rest there in company with the cook. There is also there the ghost of a small child who died by being scalded to death when boiling water was accidentally poured over him.

Nowadays, the baby plays mostly on the stairs of the sleeping quarters. One day he will return to earth and he will come as another body and another person. The sad part about this incident is that it was intended to pour cold water on him for washing, but very hot water was used instead by mistake. The mother's name began with a G and I believe there is documentation about him and the event still preserved somewhere.

Chillingham Castle, Northumberland

Chillingham Castle is alleged to be the most haunted of the many haunted castles in the whole of Britain. The main ghost that is most often seen is known as The Blue Boy and is heard to cry out in fear or agony or both as the hour of midnight approaches. Afterwards, light in the shape of a halo appears on an old four poster bed or moving in the more remote parts of the buildings.

The second ghost, claimed to be Lady Mary Berkeley, is a woman left broken-hearted when her adored husband ran off with her sister. She haunts the area around the main turret stairwell and people claim that they can hear the rustle of her dress as she passes. What is the truth?

No wonder they say it is so haunted. It is. The little boy does haunt the castle. He was only a serving boy. He was murdered while wearing the blue-coloured uniform he wore when working. That's what he always appears in. Two men held him down and molested him, then one of them stabbed him. They were bribed to do this and it was in payment for something he had done wrong.

Lady Mary Berkeley is not the woman haunting the castle nowadays. That lady has long since died and passed over peaceably. The haunting is done by the woman who was mother to the murdered boy. She wants to be with him and won't leave him. The boy does not want to leave the castle until everything is put right. He feels that everything should be put right first. But that is never going to happen. So he and his mother are still there, often together.

There is also a third person haunting the castle. He is a tall man and, when he was alive, he was very wealthy. Even now he appears to some and when he does, they can hear money jingling in his pockets as this was a habit of his when alive. He was a man who loved wealth and lived to make money and more money. At one stage, he wanted to buy some land from a neighbour and thought he could get it cheap. But the servant boy overheard the plans and let the secret become known.

That stopped the deal going through and the land was soon sold later to someone else and for a lot more money than the man had expected to pay. This was why the boy was killed. He stopped the man from making a successful deal, and in punishment and revenge the man had him murdered.

There is yet another spirit still haunting the castle. She is an elderly lady who wears a long nightdress and short, thick socks. She has lovely white hair and beautiful skin. She often walks about with a baby boy in her arms. The baby was her own stillborn child and she still loves him very deeply. When they are together, she walks around all parts of the castle and emits a glow of light. It is that brightness that people sometimes see moving about in quiet corners.

Outside the castle, in the grounds, there is yet another spirit that is still earthbound. He doesn't haunt within the castle as he never used to go in there. He was a farm worker who was buried in a field quite near the walls. His bones are still there. He was a short man who always walked with a stoop. He is never seen inside the castle itself.

A clairvoyant should go to the castle to contact the Blue Boy. It must be explained that there is no longer any reason for the boy to stay there. He should be persuaded to move on. The point is that the boy, after what happened to him, is due for a second chance at life. If he doesn't move on, he will just stay there in the castle and haunting it forever.

He is young and does not understand this. If he is not advised, he will just go on an on staying there for all time. He needs to let go and move to the spirit world so that his second chance will come. Some clairvoyant should do this out of kindness and as a duty of professional responsibility.

An apparition known as The Brown Lady is supposed to haunt Raynham Hall in Norfolk, England. There exists a famous photo said to be of her taken in 1936 by two professional photographers. Does she exist, and, if so, who was she?

She exists. The Brown Lady is the ghost of the woman who was brought to the house as a five-year-old child in the early 1800s as she was daughter of a lady who gained employment there as a senior housekeeper. She eventually followed her mother into service in the house and by the age of twenty-eight was in charge of the whole house as the housekeeper.

She later got the job after the death of her mother from cancer in her early fifties. Her father had been a gardener on the estate before dropping dead in the grounds at the age of fifty-seven years, and she, too, also married a gardener who worked at Raynham Hall.

This ghost roams around the house and gardens with her husband. Her parents have not remained at the house. The reason for the haunting is that the woman really loved her position as housekeeper. She feels not only attached to the house, but dependent on it.

As a result, she feels she still wants to take care

of the house. She roams the house both night and day. She pauses and looks around and checks things because she believes that she is still in charge of its running. This ghost will not harm anyone as she is a thoroughly good spirit. It's just that she does not wish to progress to the spirit world as she is so very happy at the house.

This couple had a son. When the Brown Lady died at a surprisingly young age, the little boy was adopted, at the age of five years, by the family who owned the house and he afterwards lived there most of the time. He was brought up as if he was their own child and he did not remember his earlier life.

The Headless Cross

The original cross was built in the 14th century in Nuns Green, Derby in England. In the 15th century, it lost its top and was later moved to a safer position in Arboretum Park, Derby, where it still stands. Two ghosts have been known to haunt this cross, one of a dog and another of a woman dressed in either grey or white. When she is seen, she appears to be walking right out of the stone. Is this true?

There is a spirit that often visits and sits on the stone. Sometimes, people say they see her in grey and white, but that is probably a trick of the light as she actually only appears in white. She also brings with her on occasions a small black-and-white terrier-type of dog that was her friend during her life. She often visits the stone to be there with her son, who died aged about twenty-five years old.

In earlier times, the cross was believed to be a healing stone. Both the woman and her son were taken to the stone to be healed, as many, many sick people were in those times. But that time the healing did not work for them and they died anyway. The woman returns to the stone to remember and to be with her son, who is resting in the spirit world, but who also returns and spends time nearby.

It is the stone at the top which has meaning. It gives out power at night and this is due to the granite inside of it. The stone still has some healing powers to this day and is blessed by the heavenly spirits. In addition, this spot is a very good meeting place for spirits so it is not impossible that others may occasionally be seen.

The Headless Horseman

A headless horseman has been seen riding along the road from Onecote across Butterton Moor to Warslow in the English Peak District. There is a question as to whether this ghost is possibly just a pedlar or is he a headless knight, killed in battle and carried home by his horse? Can you sort out the puzzle?

This is the ghost of a gardener. He rides across the moor on a white horse. The horse later died from a broken front right leg. There are so many stories of apparitions that are 'headless.' Most are false and the headless bits seem to have been added somewhere or other to make the story more 'ghostly.' This ghost, for example, although he does exist is not really headless, but merely huddled in a cloak and trying to hide his identity.

He was troubled with a habitual perversion and was ashamed of this. His family have disowned him for his behaviour with young boys and he is forced endlessly to ride the moors. He is not denied entry to Heaven, but his family will not welcome him into their group due to the shame he has brought upon them. He therefore rides the moors until forgiven.

The Headless Ghost of Stoke Hall

In Stoke Hall, Derbyshire, England, in 1880, a witness actually saw the ghost of a lady in a beautiful gown descending the stairs. She appeared to have no head. Is there any truth is this tale?

Yes. This lady was a servant who was murdered in the grounds of the property for stealing rings and other jewellery from her employers. She was murdered by the friend of another servant who was blamed for the theft of the jewellery. She does have a head, but she walks with her head turned away as she is ashamed of what she did.

The person who murdered her did so in the grounds of the house where she lived and worked. The murder was revenge for his friend, who had been imprisoned for the theft. Her body still lies buried in a hidden grave in the grounds of the estate.

The Twelve Headless Horsemen

In Shady Lane, near Thornbridge Hall, Derbyshire, it is claimed that twelve headless coffin-bearers travel along the lane bearing an empty coffin. It is said the coffin is there for the person who is unfortunate enough to meet them on their journey. Are they really there and can they cause death?

These ghosts do exist, but they are not headless and there are only two of them. They were brothers who died of a disease related to their heart and chest. They died very close together in time, about a maximum of a year apart. This fact should be noted in parish records. They still walk up and down the lane together as this is where they played as children.

They do not carry a coffin, but they both carry a roll of cloth made of the identical material that was used to cover their own coffins when they were buried. They are happy spirits and very harmless, and they watch people go by and laugh at them when they believe there are twelve of them. The idea that you might die because you see them is ghost story nonsense. They often visit the area on a Monday for some reason that is both personal and important to them.

The Headless Horseman, Manifold Valley

In Manifold Valley, Derbyshire, during the 1930s, a local resident told that he had seen a man with no head riding at a gallop on a horse. Was there really anything there to see?

Yes. This is the spirit that rides a horse and wears a long cloak with a hood that hides his head. Once again, the spirit is not really headless. It is the spirit of a holy man who used to ride the valley giving sermons, praying and seeking money and donations for both the church and for his personal use.

He died very unexpectedly and the spirits have told us that he was murdered. He was stabbed in the back in order to steal the money that he was usually known to carry, even though it was only a small amount. He rides up and down looking for the spirit of the murderer who killed him, but he will not find him.

The Haunted Mansion, Stockholm, Sweden

At the Palace of Scheffler in Stockholm is a fine house known as 'The haunted mansion.' It was built in the 1690s and has many ghostly stories attributed to it. They say strange music and other sounds are heard, and mirrors and windows have been broken for no apparent cause.

The owner was said to have had connections with the Devil and was taken away in a black carriage by the coachmen, who had horns and a tail. One couple were bricked up in the basement, and the priest who tried to exorcise the poltergeist was thrown out of a window on the upper floor. Can this all be true?

There is a graveyard near to where this palace was built and this is why the mansion is haunted. It is a common occurrence where buildings have been placed over or near to forgotten burial areas. The mansion is now particularly haunted by two people that they found down in the cellar. They were not bricked up, but they did die there and were buried in a small family tomb alongside the basement.

There is also a lady in her thirties who died there after losing her baby girl child. She is very happy and peaceful. The child died at the age of only three weeks and the woman stays there with her other child, a son.

It is pure myth that a priest was pushed out of a window when alone in the house. It's true that a priest did once die in a fall out of a window, but not that he was pushed. The truth is that one of the ghostly spirits in the house came up behind him and the intense cold and the sudden appearance of a shadowy figure was such a shock to him that he fell or jumped out of the window as he was so frightened. It was not a deliberate act by the ghost.

It is all nonsense about the Devil and the horns and tails. This house is not haunted by bad spirits in the main building. There are several ghosts altogether in the house, the small boy and his mother, the two people who were buried in the cellar, the woman with the baby, and a tall, thin man who was very ill when he died.

He was in his early sixties when he died and he was a handyman at the house who came and worked there as and when he was needed. He died in the house, although the people there had taken great care of him when he was ill.

The house is a lovely and peaceful place with happy ghosts who will not cause anyone any harm whatsoever.

The Ghost of Belgrave Hall, located in Leicester, England

Alleged to have been haunted for many years, the building now houses a museum and staff there claim to regard the several 'ghosts' as frequent, familiar and harmless. In December 1998, an apparition was caught on the security cameras and the picture has been shown throughout the world. Was this apparition a ghost?

This property is haunted by a whole family, and there are not just the group that have been spoken of, but a further four as well. The bright lights that are seen are spirits, not ghosts. However, there is a very pleasant and kind ghost of an old lady who walks the grounds and she was – and is – very happy in this house as all her family are buried nearby. She was very happy in the house with her sisters and family, and she continues to be happy there with them. She does not want to move on.

Only three ghosts appear at any one time; the others are just spirits of the family who talk with them and wish to be with them. The three ghosts walk alongside each other up and down the stairs, causing them to creak. There seems to be a meeting-place at the top of the stairs, which we believe was once a library, where everyone congregated and discussed family business. They still hold their meetings at the same times that they regularly did when they were alive.

There is also the ghost of a young girl that was a servant in the kitchen. She, too, died in the house, but again she is happy and harmless. There are also three male ghosts who stay in the grounds and we believe that they worked on the land for the family. They do not enter the house, as they did not do so in their lifetime.

There are also the ghosts of several dogs around the property. In particular, there is a tall hunting dog who runs through the grounds. He once belonged to the master of the house. These ghosts and spirits will not harm anyone at all and no attempt should be made to remove or disturb them. If they want to move, they will in their own time.

Arreton Manor, located on the Isle of Wight, has a ghostly history. Count Slade de Pomeroy, the owner of the manor, heard a tapping noise on his bedroom door. He would never open the door because on one occasion when he did, he was shoved backwards by the door opening. Yet when he looked out again, there was no-one on the other side.

His housekeeper happened to be present at the time and she said she saw two monks enter the room, one of them apparently leading the owner from the doorway before they both disappeared. There are also tales of a brutal murder having taken place there. Additionally, visitors have told of seeing a small girl wandering about and crying out for her mother. Did anything really happen here?

The little girl in the legend does haunt the house, but quite happily. She should have inherited the house, but did not, so she remains there to try and take what should rightfully have been hers. She is determined to keep her brothers out of the property to this day.

The ghost allows her brothers to stay in the roof of the property and they try to keep away from her so that she can carry on looking after the house. She is a very disturbed spirit and she does not want to go anywhere away from the house apart from the front steps. She will probably stay in the house for eternity and will be seen by many time and time again.

There are also the ghosts of two monks in the manor buildings and they are there to keep the peace between the family members. They were friends of the family and lived nearby. The monks are there to protect the girl, who does not realise that her brothers could – and would – harm her. This is why they were leading the owner away from the scene.

The girl is often seen looking out of the window of the house, and often on a very dark, quiet and still night, she can be seen sitting on the front steps. She is not sad, but she wants the house to herself.

The Ghost of Hampton Court Palace in London

Once the home of Henry VIII, and known as one of the most haunted places in Britain, security camera footage taken in October 2003 showed the image of a man opening two heavy doors. This happened three times in all and the person was dressed in period costume. So who was this man and why did he open the doors?

There is a figure of a man in a doorway and he then goes out into the yard to allow stores to be brought into the building. In his day, the man was a sort of caretaker and storekeeper, who dealt with any goods that were delivered to the palace. He opens and shuts these particular doors as this was his job in his lifetime, but he walks straight through many others.

He is the only ghost in this building and has a fascinating time opening and shutting the doors. Over time, this building has changed, which is why he opens and shuts some doors, but passes through others. It's because some of the doors have been closed up and others opened. They are not still in the same places. He spends a lot of time standing by a large fireplace and also sitting looking out of an upstairs window onto the palace grounds.

This is a good spirit who likes to stay in this particular building alone. He seems to think that it is his as he lived in that building in his lifetime when he worked at the palace. There are no other spirits in the palace and there is no-one groaning or shrieking as some have claimed.

Loftus Hall, in County Wexford, Ireland

This unusual building has a story to it which is very daunting. It is supposedly haunted by the Devil himself. On a night of bad weather, a man on horseback arrived at the house and asked to stay

the night. He was invited to join the family to play
cards. One daughter, during the game, dropped a
card under the table.

   As she bent to retrieve the card, she looked at the
visitor's feet and they resembled cloven hooves. The
girl screamed and the visitor shot up through the
roof in a puff of smoke, leaving a large hole in the
ceiling, which they have never been able to repair
properly since. What is all this about?

A helpful ghost came to the house on the night in
question in order to try and prevent a tragedy in the
family. This ghost is still around the grounds of the
house to this day. He had lived in a house nearby
with his wife, who worked in Loftus Hall. He haunts
the house to be near to her as her spirit also still
remains in the house.

There was a hatch in the ceiling that the ghost
tried to rise through when the daughter became
frightened by his presence. He did not have hooves
and there is no such being as the Devil. However, he
may have shown himself to be a ghost in some way
and this frightened the daughters of the house, who
started to scream.

In all the pandemonium that followed, the ghost
tried to rise up and away from what was happening,
but for some reason, he was unable to go through the
hatch in the ceiling of the room. There had once been
an opening such as a stairway there previously, but
for some reason, the layout of the house had changed
and his efforts to get through the hatch caused burn
marks to appear around it.

The important thing that happened on that night
was that no harm came to the family due to the
protection of the ghost. At the time, he wanted the

family to move to a safer part of the house because he believed that the storm was to have been far worse than it actually was, and that lightning may have struck the house and caused a fire in which the family could have died.

Chapter 13

A FEW FAMOUS CRIMINALS

Jack the Ripper brought terror to the local residents in the East End of London from 1888 to 1891 when he carried out a series of horrific murders that still remain unsolved. Who was he?

[Note from Laurie James: During the contact sessions we had, while collecting data on this famous murderer, I was surprised and shocked when spirits other than Lilian, my mother, began to intervene and seek to pass on information. At least two of these spirits were victims of the murderer and were able to give first-hand accounts of what actually happened. Wilf later explained to me that there is nothing unusual in other spirits joining in when they either hear something of interest or something of which they have knowledge.]

Jack the Ripper was a short man with a scarred face. He had a deformed, rather flattened nose and his victims describe him as snorting or breathing heavily through it at times and particularly so when he was murdering his victims. He was a cobbler by trade and had his own small shop and workroom. According to one of his victims, he was always of the opinion that he was very clever, but in reality this was very far from the truth.

Apart from the murders and the evil deeds that he did to women, which is the reason for his being famous, he was in reality a very kind man. His parents had deserted him when he was young and this, along with the fact that his father had also been murdered, affected him badly. He had admired his father very much. His father's name was George and he had been named after him. Jack was only a nickname.

Jack had a small shop and workshop just two or three doors away from a street corner. On the corner of the street, there was a lamppost and also a post box. It was in a seedy area of London where prostitutes would frequent the streets at night. It was common for the prostitutes to work around corners and lampposts, where they loitered looking for trade.

Mary Ann Nichols, one of his victims, told us that Jack had been involved in the arrangement of – or the carrying out – abortions on women in his past. He helped young girls to get rid of their unwanted pregnancies. Mary herself had already had two pregnancies aborted and she used Jack's services on both occasions.

Jack did not kill just any prostitute; he carefully selected his victims. He held nothing against his victims personally. It was the fact that they were prostitutes that mattered to him. He used prostitutes for his personal needs, but despised what they did for a living. Jack's victims were always girls who had been pregnant and had undergone abortions. He felt that abortions were very wrong. Therefore, he selected his victims from those prostitutes that knew to have had abortions.

He used to kill his carefully selected victims and cut parts of their womb out of them. He did this because he believed that if he cut such body parts out of them, then if they were to return by reincarnation, which is something that he believed in, they would not be able to have children again. He was very hypocritical as he took money for helping women to have abortions, but he despised them all deep down for what they did. However, he also used the abortions as a way of finding his victims and gaining their confidence.

Although the Ripper had a deformity in his right shoulder, he was a reasonable tradesman and worked hard to make a living. He mostly remained in the tiny workshop at the back of his shop and would only come out to the front to attend to customers. He did most of his cobbling in the workshop, where he also had a bed. He could not abide being with small children as he felt himself to be unreliable with them, especially little boys. Just a few months after killing his last victim, he was taken ill and was admitted to his local hospital, where he died shortly after.

The reason that Jack the Ripper was never caught was because he was very cunning. He would always arrange to meet his proposed victims beforehand, and sometimes several times. He never just killed someone whom he came upon in a quiet, lonely street and entirely by chance. He always knew when and where he was going to meet them. Twice he picked the same area and the same place. He used to check the area out first to ensure that he would not be disturbed or found out. He would take his victim to the predetermined place for his evil deed.

He would first strike them a heavy blow on the head or shoulder. This would knock them down. He needed them on the ground as he was not a large man and needed to get them down on the floor to do his butchering tasks. After he had murdered his victim, he would be very distraught for a while and was very often physically sick. However, during the time that he was butchering these unfortunate women, he enjoyed the thrill of it and also having power over them.

[One victim actually told Wilf, while I was there listening, that she had lain in her coffin wondering whether the truth would ever come out and has been hoping above all that it would. J.L.]

George, which we believe to be his real name, was of two different nationalities. The reason the police could not catch him was that he planned the times and locations for his murders very carefully and would visit them several times to become familiar with them. He would also visit his selected locations at different times of the day as he wanted to ensure that he would not be caught or disturbed.

His usual way was to approach the prostitutes while they were on their afternoon rounds and arrange to meet them either that evening or on another day. He also killed women other than those whose murder he has been credited with, but the police never realised the true extent of his crimes. If anyone takes the trouble to check now, they will find that at least four other women were strangled, but not mutilated during the year before he became so notorious. He also selected his victims for their looks. He particularly liked girls with rounded noses, high cheekbones and dark hair.

Mary Jane Kelly told us that she was killed very quickly. Previously, she had already undergone two abortions, but desperately wanted a child. She had a boyfriend who was very kind to her, but he was already married. She is happy and very contented now in the spirit world.

However, she still feels this man should be named and shamed, even though he passed over so long ago. They have not seen him in the spirit world and they do not want to. They believe he is in a different country caring for his present family members, possibly in Germany.

Mary Kelly was having trouble with her ankle when she was murdered, and it was bandaged to give it support. It would be interesting to check the medical records on file to see whether this was mentioned in the crime report. Mary Kelly and her friends hope that this information will help anyone who investigates this matter further in order to find out the man's last name. They believe that his surname started with the letter T.

Annie Chapman, another victim, was a lovely person who was liked by everyone. She very much fitted the description of Jack's favoured round nose and dark hair. She very strong-willed and had a forceful personality. Annie had also had three abortions, but had, in addition, given birth to two children. She was ill at the time of her death and was receiving treatment from her doctor for stomach pains. As well as her night-time activity as a prostitute, she also had an ordinary daytime job, which did not pay much money and probably forced her to work as a prostitute to keep a roof over her children's head.

Jack had approached Annie three times before and she had previously had sex with him. It was the same with all of Jack's victims. He had sex with them before deciding whether to murder them or not. He did not have sex with his victims at the times of the killings as he was afraid the time factor involved in the murder would make the chance of his being discovered so much greater. On the particular day that he arranged to meet Annie, it was raining.

At the pre-arranged time and location, he approached her and hit her hard on the head with something that he had in his coat. She does not remember anything more apart from looking down and seeing her body being butchered by Jack, who she describes as the horrible, wrinkled man who was taking a piece out of her body. Annie had always feared for her life because of her work as a prostitute, but this was more dreadful than anything she could have imagined. The Ripper had one special favourite woman, a prostitute named Jane Morris. He did not kill her and he used to see her about twice a week.

Jack the Ripper has heard about the writing of this book even in the spirit world. After all these years, he still does not want his name to be exposed because of the shame to his existing descendants. Some of them are abroad, but others are still living in London quite near to where he carried out his murders. During his life, he was a sad and unhappy man. Apart from the deformity that he had in his shoulder, he also had a physical problem with one foot and that made him limp slightly. Jack was very ashamed of his physical deformities and appearance.

[Note from Wilf Truscott, clairvoyant: Mary Jane Kelly's spirit visited me and said that Jack the Ripper was 'a rotten bastard' and did not need to do what he did to her. In my experience, it is very rare for a spirit to say anything so vindictive.]

I feel that the location of the shop and workshop where Jack the Ripper lived and worked is in the Whitechapel area of East London. The shop was separated into two parts by a curtain. There was also an upstairs that was not used as it was in a bad state of repair and the roof leaked.

All the women who were Jack's victims had actually visited him at his shop at some time or another. Jack lived and worked within easy walking distance of where the prostitutes were and also near to the locations where he committed the murders. His shop premises are still there today, and I believe that they are in the area of Commercial Road in East London.

Lord Lucan, a British nobleman, was suspected of the murder of the family nanny by allegedly battering her to death at the family home. Afterwards, he left the house and was never seen again. What is the truth of this mystery?

The nanny of Lord Lucan's children was blackmailing him over an affair he was having with another woman. The affair was with a young, dark haired woman, who was then in her early thirties. I have spoken to the spirit of Lord Lucan and at first he was very reluctant to talk about the matter. However, he has since decided that he does now want the truth to be known.

He had a confrontation with the family nanny and this developed into a heated argument. He lost his temper and in a fit of uncontrollable rage, he battered her to death. The reason for the argument was because she was threatening to tell his wife about his affair with the other woman unless he paid her an immediate sum of money to keep her quiet. At that time, he had financial problems that meant he could not pay the nanny off straight away. Unfortunately, she did not believe him at that time, so he just snapped and battered her to death.

His wife happened to return home unexpectedly just after he had killed the nanny. Therefore, he did not have time to decide what to do to cover his tracks or to dispose of the body. Due to the state of panic that he was in, he flew into an uncontrollable rage with his wife, which led to him also attacking her.

Fortunately for Lady Lucan, he was interrupted by a noise upstairs, which stopped him from beating her to death as well. He then fled from the house, got into his car and drove off. He then decided to go to two friends in Uckfield and to ask for their help and for somewhere to stay. However, he felt unable to stay there as it would have been unsafe for them to be found by the police harbouring a murderer. He therefore left their house shortly afterwards and drove down to the port of Newhaven in Sussex.

When he got there, he sat contemplating his actions and wondering what he should do. He decided that he would commit suicide by gassing himself with car fumes, but then changed his mind for the sake of his family.

Lord Lucan left his car and jumped on board a small boat moored in the port and stole it. He thought that he was a good sailor and therefore decided to sail out to sea to try and clear his head. He was contemplating whether to return to land and to give himself up to the authorities and to also confess to the murder of the nanny and the attack on his wife. Financially, he also knew he would be ruined and that there was little hope that the public would remain on his side after what he had done.

He found a bottle of spirits on the boat and he started drinking and thinking about what he had done. This caused him to be even more distressed and he started to cry. Earlier that evening, he had taken some sleeping pills, so these mixed with the alcohol meant that he became quite drowsy.

When the boat was a short distance from the shore, he started having trouble with the boat. The boat seemed to be going round in large circles. He climbed to the top deck to try and see what the problem was, but he slipped in his drowsy state, banged his head on the deck and rolled into the sea. He was too drunk and drowsy to swim to save himself.

The boat was still moving and he could not catch up with it. He was not wearing a life jacket and as a result, he drowned very quickly. The currents quickly carried his body out to sea and away from the area where people started to search for him. His body was eaten by the fish.

The boat was later found abandoned, the wind and tide having changed and brought it back into towards land, and it was assumed merely to have slipped its mooring. No connection was ever made with the disappearance of Lord Lucan.

In Heaven, he feels very sorry for what he has done and particularly how he cheated on and beat his wife, and how he murdered their nanny. They were tragic circumstances which happened on the spur of the moment. It was a situation where he overreacted to events and he regrets it now. Lord Lucan has said that he did not wake up that morning with the intention of killing or harming anyone.

He sees now that he was stupid and just hopes that everyone in his family will eventually forgive him, and when they finally join him in the spirit world, he hopes that they can all be happy together again. These are his wishes and he really does hope that his explanation will help people understand why and where he disappeared to. He still feels to this day that his drowning was the punishment for his crime, but we here know what really happened was an unfortunate accident.

He was not really a bad person; he was just a person who lost his head during the heat of the moment because he was just so frustrated and did not know which way to turn. This caused him to go into an uncontrollable rage and made him resort to lashing out. This has happened to many people in the past, but fortunately most have managed to control their temper. Even in extreme cases, they did not go so far as to kill someone.

What is the truth about the supposed sightings of 'Spring heeled Jack' in London in 1837?

He was a human being, who has now passed into the spirit world. During his lifetime, he carried out a variety of criminal acts including theft, assault and rape, but always avoided capture by the police due to his great agility. It was this agility that gave him his name, but the reality was that he was jumping from one object to another object and not just from the ground.

However, he was capable of leaping very high in the air, and on occasions he wore a tight fitting helmet, black cape and some other form of tight clothing, which was very similar to an oilskin. This gave him a very strange appearance and made people believe that was some sort of superhuman being deriving his powers direct from the Devil.

He picked his victims very carefully with the aim of robbing them or otherwise harming them. He was also a sexually frustrated man due to the fact that he was, as we would say today, impotent because his genitals were not properly formed. This further motivated him in his life of crime.

This man lived to the age of fifty-two years. He had back problems and stopped his attacks on women when he was forty. After that, he devoted his attentions mostly to men and to robbery. He has said that he attacked eight different women and that he liked to dress up in different costumes when he carried out the assaults.

At various times, he dressed up as a clown, a priest in a cloak and so on. Women were wary of him and did not like him because of his disfigured face and frightening looks. In those days, people were very superstitious and had closed minds.

He was not shot by soldiers in 1870 as is rumoured. Nor was he a reincarnation of the Devil as the superstition goes. There is no such creature as the Devil.

Chapter 14

OUR HUMAN JOURNEY
AND ITS REASONS EXPLAINED

Do the spirits have a general message for humans?

Whatever happens in our life on earth as human beings, whether it be happy, sad, fearful or tragic, it is all very important. It is all part of the learning process that we go through in our lifetime. Throughout our lives, we build on our personal experiences and are better people for many of the things that happen to us.

We entered the physical world through the first tunnel, our mother's birth canal, and we have all the feelings, emotions and intelligence that a young animal would have. Our physical body and young spirit grow together throughout our younger years. Our bodies generally mature by the age of twenty-one years or even younger in some individuals, but our spirit matures at the age of twenty-seven years.

At the time of our death, our spirit then discards its earthly body, which is no longer needed. It then passes through the second tunnel and enters into Heaven, the kingdom of God. During our earthly life, we produce more children who, in turn, will follow our path towards enlarging God's spiritual kingdom.

Although Heaven extends from the earth's surface to the highest mountain tops, most of the active spirits stay on the lower levels to look after their loved ones in the earthly world.

If you die before your twenty-seventh birthday, you will come to heaven to wait for your second human life. In your second life, the spirits will try to ensure that you live a longer life.

Once you reach the age of twenty-seven years old, God considers you to be a fully developed mature spirit. Once you pass over after this age, no matter what age you may be, you are not expected to return in human form again. Instead, you will find the true and unbelievable eternal happiness that we all experience here in Heaven.

Once you have been to Heaven, there are not many spirits who would wish for any further earthly lives. There is no way that I would personally ever want to go back through the tunnel and become human again. Life as a spirit here in Heaven is so much better than life as a human being.

Chapter 15

HOW AND WHY THE BOOK WAS WRITTEN
Author's Comments

I asked Wilf if he could explain why this book is a first in its field and how we were in such a unique position to be able to compile all of this previously undisclosed information.

Wilf replied by explaining that it was due entirely to my mother, Lilian, and that she was the most powerful and willing spirit he had ever encountered during more than thirty years as a practising clairvoyant.

I was quite amazed at his reply because when she was in the physical world, she was just my mother and was in no other way any different from so many of her generation who had lived through bad times. She married my father, Ernest James, during the Second World War. They had four children – two boys and two girls.

I can only imagine that her strength and resolve were derived from the tragedies that beset her earlier on in life. The first tragedy occurred when a bomb landed and exploded next to the house where my mother and father were staying at the time. There was an explosion and my father rushed over to her and acted as a human shield to protect her from the falling debris.

At that time, my mother was heavily pregnant with the child that turned out to be my older sister. There is no doubt that his swift actions protected her, but my father paid a high price for his selfless action. He suffered multiple injuries, including being hit on the head, and it was the damage he sustained from that head injury that sadly turned out to be the start of many future problems for him.

The next tragedy occurred when my sister Sandra was just three years old. The gate in the front garden had been accidentally left open. Sandra ran out into the busy main road and was knocked down and killed outright by a motor cyclist, who did not even stop. Shortly after this sad event, my father's mother passed over, adding to the family's grief.

Through the hard times of the war, my father was less resilient than my mother, as the tragic deaths of my sister and paternal grandmother had started to take their toll on him. They affected his mental health and he had been forced to start taking medication for his nervous problems. Despite the tragedies that had beset my family, my parents expanded the family with me being the next born, and then along came my brother David and finally my sister Glynis.

By the time I reached the age of eight years in the early 1950s, my father was finding it very hard to cope. The strain of losing his first child, Sandra, so tragically had really affected his mental health and he just could not cope. Finally, my parents separated and he left us and went to live with his sister, who was able to care for him on a fulltime basis without the added stress caused by three young boisterous children. Consequently, my mother faced the further hardship of having to bring up three children on her own in a society that was still scathing of separation and divorce.

My mother was very proud when I passed my common entrance (Eleven-plus) examination and I was accepted at Abbs Cross Technical School in Hornchurch, Essex. Five years later, my mother had a further reason to be proud of me when at the age of sixteen, I won a scholarship for training with a major British car manufacturer as a trainee body design engineer.

Seven years later, at the age of twenty-three, I left that position and went to work for a private auto design centre in Detroit, USA, which was a wonderful opportunity for me. My next career move was to a car manufacturer in Munich in Germany, and only three years later I was able to start my own car design company. Within ten years of starting-up on my own, I had design centres located in six countries and I employed over four hundred design engineers.

I retired from business in 2000 and was living quietly in Hornchurch. By that time, I had separated from my wife, and through the boredom of living on my own, I started to consider the possibility of living abroad once again. A long-term friend of mine, who had retired and taken up residence in Paphos in Cyprus, telephoned me and invited me to go and visit him for a holiday. I was curious to know why this particular island had appealed to him, so I booked a flight and flew over to see him.

I was immediately struck by the friendly atmosphere and hospitality shown by the locals in this little seaside resort in the sun. It seemed to me that if there was a Utopia, this was exactly how I would imagine it to be. In no time I was hooked! So I flew back to England, sold my house – complete with furniture – packed my bags and moved to Paphos.

In July 2005, my sister Glynis telephoned me to say that she was very concerned about our mother, who had been taken ill and admitted to hospital. Glynis feared the worst and considered that our mother's medical condition was both extremely serious and potentially terminal.

My brother and sisters' heavy work commitments meant that they were only able to visit our mum in the evenings and this concerned me greatly. Consequently, I flew back to England immediately and went straight to the hospital from the airport. During the week that followed, my mother, despite being very ill, complained constantly to me about the poor quality and lack of taste and appeal of the hospital food. She also felt strongly that the attention given to the patients by the nurses was both very poor and minimal.

Due to her complaints about the food she was being given, I started making her meals at home and taking them in to her at the hospital. However, this still was not enough for her as she just wanted to go home to be with her family for the precious time that she had left to her and she did not care about her illness or treatments for it.

After long negotiations with both the nursing and medical staff, the hospital reluctantly agreed to allow me take her home. I was handed all my mother's medicines, a Zimmer frame and a wheelchair, and I wheeled her out of the hospital and drove her home. She was so happy to be back in her own home. The look on her face said it all. I knew she had not lost her wonderful sense of humour when she stated 'They would have killed me if I had stayed in there any longer!'

During the next few days, my mother's health seemed to improve to such a degree that I felt sure that she was recovering and on the mend. Unfortunately, I had some unfinished business commitments in Paphos that demanded urgent attention, but as mum appeared to be so much better, I decided that it would be safe to take the risk to return to Cyprus for a few days.

I told mum that I would be back very soon to continue to nurse her back to health and I flew back to Paphos. Two days later, my sister phoned me with the dreadful news that our mother had suffered a fatal relapse and that as a result of this, she had been readmitted to hospital and had passed away on 12th August, 2005.

I was both heartbroken at losing my mother and felt very guilty for leaving her and that I should have stayed at home with her. In particular, she had always been there for me when I needed her, but I was not there for her when it really mattered, when she needed me in her dying moments. I felt so sad that I did not stay with her and that I had missed the opportunity to hold her hand for the last time or to say goodbye to her, thank her for everything and tell her that I loved her very much.

Even though we all know it is inevitable that our parents will die some day, we never expect it to happen. Somehow, we manage to convince ourselves that they will live forever. Even after the tragic event of the death of a parent, it is still hard to come to terms with and accept it. We tend to reproach ourselves for what we did not do in their lifetime and start to think about how things should have been and what we should have done if at all humanly possible to ensure that we were with them when they finally passed over. It all seems so easy in hindsight, but the practicalities of modern life mean that very often we are many thousands of miles apart.

I took the next available flight back to the UK, attended mum's funeral and then returned again to my new life in Paphos. As I had now lost my mother forever, or as I thought at the time, I had to come to terms with the fact that I would never see her again, never talk to her again or have any contact whatsoever with her. Death was final, or so I believed at the time, but I was so wrong!

In April 2006, I met Wilf Truscott, the West Country clairvoyant, and his wife Jeanette in an office I was temporarily borrowing from a friend to finalise the designs of an invention I had been working on in my retirement to alleviate boredom, keep me occupied and to help me get over the loss of my mother.

Wilf explained that he, his wife and their three dogs had come over to Paphos to semi-retire and were just waiting for the completion of their new house that they had purchased. We hit it off as friends immediately and were amazed to find out that we even had the same birthday of 16th April. However, as Wilf frequently reminds me, he is one year younger than me!

Since that day, whenever we refer to our birthdays, he has always taken the opportunity to humorously proclaim that he is the younger of the two of us! Wilf told me the following story about his life and what brought about the realisation of his gift of clairvoyance.

Wilf Truscott, was born in Plymouth in Devon on 16th April, 1947, and comes from a long line of clairvoyants. He was strongly drawn to the island of

Cyprus following a brief visit in 2004 and eventually moved there permanently in April 2006.

Originally, his family comes from Cornwall around the St Ives area, and Truscott is a very old and well-known Cornish name. The story that is handed down through Wilf's family is that the family come from Cornish gypsies and tinkers, and that there were many gifted clairvoyants in the family. In particular, Wilf's great-grandmother on his father's side of the family was a gifted clairvoyant.

Wilf is one of six children and the first boy after three daughters for his parents Marjorie and Bill. His father passed away with asbestosis contracted from working in the Plymouth Dockyard when Wilf was in his early thirties. Wilf had brought his father home from hospital to die and physically carried him out of the ward against medical advice. His father was pleased to be home and to have his family around him.

Wilf visited him the following day and his last words to Wilf before he left the house were 'You will be a healer, my son.' Wilf became very upset at these words as he knew his father was very near to death and he left the room. Unfortunately, he did not see his father alive again as he died only hours later before Wilf was able to get back to see him.

From that time on, Wilf has developed healing powers that have grown stronger over the years – a gift that has helped many, many people. In particular, it is always Wilf's father who is with him when he is healing and he always knows he is present because he starts yawning and that is the sign that he is there helping him. At the same time, other spirits that belong to the person undergoing healing will also be there to help Wilf and his father.

When Wilf was a child, if asked what he wanted to be when he grew up, he would always answer 'Twenty-seven years old.' This strange response was finally explained when he reached that age and was told by an elderly clairvoyant friend of the family, Connie, that he had the gift of second sight or clairvoyance. This, in turn, explained the many strange things that had happened to him over the years. Connie helped Wilf to develop, use and cherish his gift until her early death only eight weeks later.

One day, Connie sent for Wilf, told him that she was ill and asked that he visit her in hospital. Wilf then told her that she would be out of pain in three days' time. At that time, Connie asked Wilf to take something of hers to remember her by and to this day one of his most treasured possessions is a vase that she gave to him. Wilf visited Connie just before she died three days after she had sent for him. At that time, Connie explained to Wilf what he needed to do to progress his gift and powers, and that the spirits would come for him when he was ready.

Wilf became a full-time professional clairvoyant at the age of thirty-two years following a back injury, by which time he already had a following of loyal clients from his part-time activities of learning his trade over the previous four to five years. Wilf firmly believes that his injury and move to being a full-time medium was the will of the spirits.

He states that from that time he has never looked back or wanted for anything, despite taking such a risky step. He is also adamant that he has never exploited his gift, beyond making a reasonable living and fully believes that the spirits watch over and protect him at all times to enable him to carry on his work.

Apart from the gift of clairvoyance, Wilf also has very strong healing powers and has helped many people and animals over the years and particularly since his move to Cyprus. Over time, he has been able to heal people, help in the relief of pain or aid in the remission of a variety of chronic conditions.

Over the years, his gift of clairvoyance has grown, and grown to the point where he can do readings and spiritual healing from photographs and over the telephone. He has clients all over the world and given many radio interviews for the BBC in Devon and the Channel Islands, and other local radio stations.

One of Wilf's many personal successes over the years was when he appeared in a community hall in Looe, Cornwall, and the queue outside was so bad that he could not even get in to start the evening! Wilf's main ambition in life now is to do a television show incorporating live healing.

As Wilf and I became friendlier and we shared work premises, my mother started to intervene in his readings with other clients and he recognised what a strong spirit she was. As time went on, the idea for the book came about and grew from idle chatter to what you see today.

Wilf is a remarkable and unassuming character who is neither sensational nor theatrical in his professional dealings. There is not an earring or spotted scarf to be seen, but just a happy, down-to-earth person with a crystal ball.

When Wilf came into my life, I started having contact with mum through him. The thought of mum not being there still brought tears to my eyes at that point as my loss was still very recent and hard to bear. Wilf being around brought me back in contact with mum and also many thought-provoking questions that I put to him regularly.

I asked Wilf where exactly in Heaven my mother was and did she have some form of daily routine? He explained to me that Heaven is all around us and that my mother was caring for me every day. He also told me that she had said that spirits interchange with each other and take turns to look after the loved ones that they have left behind. During one of our sessions, my mother told Wilf that before she had passed on, her mother had been looking after me and that now they did it together.

Wilf can talk to the spirit world at will and there are always spirits near to him wherever he is. He told me that when he is asked to make contact with a spirit on behalf of a client, he can only do so if the spirit is with that person at the relevant time. If the spirit is present, Wilf can talk to them and pass messages both ways.

I asked Wilf whether we could get together and attempt to write this book. I was very interested in writing a spiritual version of the world's mysteries, myths, unsolved data and experiences, if it was at all possible. Wilf contacted my mother to see if it would be possible for the spirit world to collaborate on such a project. My mother felt that it would be possible with both her help and the help of spirits from all around the world.

She also said that she would be glad to take this opportunity to act as a link to the spiritual world and hopefully find the answers to all our questions. She seemed to be very excited at the proposed project and also said that she felt other spirits would also feel happy at giving information to the world. For me, this was the greatest gift that I could ever be offered. Not only the prospect of having contact with my wonderful mother again, but also to be able to have this contact with her on a regular basis.

During one of our sessions, my mother asked that Wilf and I remain long-term friends so that she could maintain a permanent contact with me, which is a wonderful gift for someone who has been bereaved and suffered the loss of a loved one. A start date was agreed and I set about compiling lists of questions to take to the regular meetings that Wilf and I held. Due to the speed at which Wilf works, it was decided that everything would be recorded in order to capture all that was said and so that the tapes could be transcribed at a later date.

We were absolutely amazed at the response from the spirit world. My mother passed the answers on to Wilf at lightning speed. When she did not know the answer, she told him to ask a few days later and she would meanwhile send another spirit off to find out.

Wilf said that never in all his years as a clairvoyant had he ever encountered such an overwhelming enthusiasm coming from so many spirits. It was far, far greater than he had ever known or thought possible. Some days he could hardly speak or think for the overwhelming number of spirits being around him. It seemed as though every spirit in Heaven had heard of the project and wanted to help. There was huge excitement about the book in the spirit world: they finally wanted the true facts known.

As they all wanted the truth to be known, the spirits were trying to smooth the way to ensure a speedy publication of the book. It was truly remarkable! The next milestone was how were we going to give the spirits' answers to our questions to the world? We needed advice on how to market the book. Therefore, I contacted an old friend of mine, Dick Richards, MD, who also lived in Paphos.

Dr Dick has written many books and had them published. He was naturally very curious about the project and asked if it would be possible to see some samples of our work, and in April 2007, the data was presented to him. In particular, I had carefully selected the items relating to biblical history as I knew that this particular subject was a real passion of his. Dr Dick reassured me he would be open-minded about the content, but it was quite obvious that he was somewhat dubious about the project.

Dr Dick's brief was to examine the answers and to get back to us when he was ready to give an honest opinion about the subject matter. One of the subjects given to him was the text relating to King Herod the Great.

A question was asked about King Herod's burial place. He was told that the location of Herod's tomb, which until then had not been discovered, was located a few miles south-east of Bethlehem. Herod was stricken with disease and believed that because of this affliction, his spirit would not be accepted into Heaven, especially if he was to be buried in a tomb. He believed that if his body were cremated, he would be accepted. Therefore, he chose cremation and requested that his ashes be spread over the sands nearby.

An excited Dr Dick telephoned me in May 2007 to inform me that the 9th May, 2007 edition of the UK's 'Daily Mail' carried a story about Dr Ehud Metzer. He was the leader of an important archaeological team who had just found the long-lost tomb of King Herod the Great. It was totally intact with no signs of forced entry and located exactly in the area where the spirits had claimed it to be – at Herodion, just five miles south-east of Bethlehem. Dr Dick was very impressed, but even more amazed when a further remarkable discovery was made by the team. When they opened Herod's sarcophagus, it was empty… just as the spirits had told us! We now had Dr Dick very firmly on board as our editor.

Readers should note that much of this book is transcribed exactly as Lilian James' words came from the clairvoyant's lips and onto the tape recorder. Apart from editing, there have been no significant changes made. Although Lilian James was relating the answers as they came to her, in certain subjects, it was clear that as she did not possess previous or well-informed knowledge. In many cases, she did not always understand the subject matter about which she was speaking. Lilian sought help from the spirit world far and wide, and with helpers travelled to get the correct information. On occasions, she went herself. At other times, she merely passed on information as it was told to her.

A closing message from Wilf

I have really enjoyed working with Laurie James and his mother Lilian, who is in the spirit world, to produce this book. Lilian and many other spirits have both encouraged and motivated us both to complete this book. Whether you share the views passed to us or not, I ask you to keep your mind open and consider its content.

It has been a wonderful learning experience for me after so many years as a clairvoyant. The knowledge of both the Bible and the mysteries of the world has been quite astounding for me personally. I hope that the readers of this work will also feel the same way.

After more than thirty years as a clairvoyant, I did not feel that I had much left to learn. Now I feel that I have learnt so much via my gift, contact with Lilian and all the other spirits that have passed on information during the time the book was in production.

I would like to thank Lilian James, the strongest spirit I have ever encountered, Phillipa James for her help with the cover and typing, and Dr Dick Richards for his help, advice, writing skills and guidance. Thanks also to my wife, Jeanette Truscott for her proof-reading, corrections and suggestions, and Laurie James for his faith in me and encouragement. Without Laurie's encouragement and guidance, I would never have contemplated such a venture.

Chapter 16

A FINAL MESSAGE FROM THE SPIRIT WORLD

This book has been written to enlighten mankind. It tells about the fact that we spirits exist and how we do, why we are here, where we are going and what we must all do, humans and spirits alike, to survive on our planet.

Those who have never believed in God will, we hope, understand better about Him after reading this book. For those who believe in and follow a particular religion, we hope it will make them have more tolerance towards other faiths and to believe that there is truly only one God.

We hope, too, that you will understand that life on our planet as we know it is desperately threatened. Future generations of children will have to be educated to understand both what is happening in the world and also what they must do to care for and respect the planet. It is vital that they learn in order to preserve it and to make their lives – and the lives of future generations – better and safer.

We also want to let you know that you must not be afraid of death when it comes as Heaven is a wonderful place. You need to try to be both kind and peaceful during your time on earth. If you are cruel and treat other humans badly – and particularly by not giving them the respect that every human deserves, regardless of nationality, colour or creed – we cannot ensure that you will be allowed to progress to being with your family and loved ones in our world as it is today.

But by following the simple paths we have shown, you will always be looked after by your spirit family, many of them from long before you were born. We love you and care for you, and we watch over every one of you. Then, when your time comes, we will help you to make the move from earthly life to the spirit world, where you will join us and other loved ones in the wonderful place called Heaven… and this will be forever. There could be no better reason for happiness, security and hope.

Conclusion

FIRST, A WARNING

A very wise man once said that the biggest trouble with people is not so much what they don't know, but what they do know that just ain't so.

Being the way we are, we humans tend to accept the things we were taught in infancy. This is a sound biological principle. If the young creature learns quickly and unquestioningly from its parents, by obeying them and following their examples, it has a far greater chance of survival in the wild. Furthermore, the things learned in the early years tend to linger on in the mind as unquestioned thoughts or certainties that are never again seriously doubted or addressed.

To the adult, the pitfalls of this system become obvious as the years progress. Nevertheless, most people still have in their minds some of the old-fashioned ideas of parents, grandparents and even far earlier influences. Many of these may well still be valid. Others may not. But one thing is usual… when those ideas are first seriously questioned, they meet an almost instinctive resistance. It is as if people do not want to change. They do not want to re-learn. They do not want to know new or different things that seem wrong. They are not open-minded enough to pause, reflect and re-think their old ideas.

The present writer, the editor, was a life-long atheist. Though I try always to remain open-minded, I had never yet found any convincing cause for belief in anything supernatural. The entirety of everything in the universe I so far find to be totally natural... perhaps not yet understood, but, nevertheless, natural for all that.

For me, to commend religious faith is to advocate irrationality. But working on this book has made even me feel my beliefs somewhat stirred, if not shaken. For this book raises serious doubts about so many things. Previously taught and long-held convictions have been questioned. New and unexpected explanations have arisen.

For decades, I have felt such a reappraisal was long overdue. So much nonsense attaches to those formal religions with which I am familiar – prophets leaping off rocks en route to heaven; virgin births; God behaving like an evil, egotistical and capricious child in the Old Testament, one single, monotheist indivisible God who is, nonetheless, in three distinct bits; maddeningly inconsistent stories and – above all, perhaps – miracles. Magic is great fun on the stage, but as we all know, it cannot really happen.

Yet by any workable definition, miracles are just that. Examples of magic – incidents where the correct course of nature is disrupted. Now things that cannot happen simply do not happen; and things that can happen and do happen are not miracles. So much nonsense is talked about religion that any educated or thinking person is likely to be insulted at the assault on his intelligence. Yet it is proclaimed and spouted from the pulpits of churches world-wide.

It's no good merely pointing out these nonsensical idiosyncrasies or standing back in amazement while a church controlled by intelligent men is frantically scratching about for miracles with which to fast-track a recently deceased Pope towards sainthood. Yet these things are happening every day.

With a lack of logic that would confound Euclid and perplex Solomon, a remarkably large proportion of people just won't, or won't be bothered, to re-learn. The prevailing attitude is 'My mind is made up. Please don't confuse me with facts!' In view of all this, I therefore find it no surprise that I have spent sixty years as a doctor, scientist and stalwart Dawkinsian-Darwinian atheist.

But now, suddenly, comes new data to which the sensible mind must always remain open. No-one is trotting it out as required belief. What is being offered is a new approach, a new series of events described not as supernatural or miraculous, but as simple truths, the logic of which is so immeasurably greater than what was before. In plain terms, to me the alternative suggestions raised make the whole concept seem like far better sense.

Foremost amongst these suggestions for this editor has been the claim that there really is a God, albeit that He is not proclaimed to be the omnipotent, loving, caring 'God Almighty' of the Bible. Far from it. Neither is He, by any means, to be alternatively equated with the Allah of the Koran or even the Jahweh, or Jehovah, of Judaism. There is one God only, the spirits say, and whatever you call Him, makes no difference and does not even remotely interest Him.

Another shock comes when the reader realises that the God of the Bible does not exist. He never does and never did communicate with humans. He never gave the Ten Commandments to the leader, Moses. In fact, Moses, as such, never existed either. What is more, God has no interest in us as humans. He does not hear, heed or respond to prayers. He has no wishes or rules for our standards of behaviour. He holds no Day of Judgement and meets out neither punishment nor reward ever or to anyone.

In other words, He is merely a powerful but aloof God of here and now, just of this planet. He is real and He exists, but is not omnipotent, omnipresent or omniscient. Nor is He the highly acclaimed Cosmocrator of the universe.

It also comes as a startling thought to learn that the concept most have of Heaven, a place where there is no such thing as democracy, is almost entirely imaginary. The idea that there is a place where angels in long flowing robes gather round a celestial throne and sing angelic strains to the flapping of wings is just not the case.

Next, the idea that Jesus was the physical son of a god is exposed as nonsense. This, of course, is something many have suspected before, but not known for sure. So is the idea that his body was physically resurrected from the grave after his death. Indeed, the theology of Judaism and Islam, both of which regard Jesus as a teacher and prophet in every way human, appear far closer to the truth than the preposterous and, by most, scarcely understood idea that he is really one integral part of the three-in-one theory of the Holy Trinity.

Jesus, as we shall hear claimed, was Mary's illegitimate child. There was no immaculate conception or a miraculous, storybook birth with shepherds and 'wise men' or stars in the East. There is no truth in the much-loved and oft-told nativity tales of the ox, the ass, the manger, the moving star of Bethlehem, the stable or the business about there being no room at the inn.

The shepherds watching their flocks by night, the visiting angels and the journeyings of the Magi are just lovely old yarns. Jesus seldom moved from Jerusalem, where he was born, lived and died. He never lived in Nazareth: he never performed miracles like walking on water, turning water into wine or literally feeding five thousand mouths on a few loaves and fishes.

The idea that he came from Nazareth was probably a historical mistake. It is suggested that the idea arose because at one time he may have become associated with an unorthodox Jewish religious order known as Nazarites. No more than that. Perhaps he was Jesus the Nazarite, not Jesus the Nazarene.

Similarly, angels do not exist in the way we have been led to believe. There are no mighty, flying creatures with haloes and long, feathered wings. But there are, as it were, 'guardian angels.' Perhaps that is somehow what has given rise to the whole idea – earth spirits who are members of our own families whose terrestrial lives are over and who are now residents of the spirit world which, for want of a better word, we have called Heaven. They certainly watch over us and help us in many unseen ways both during our lives and eventually at our certain and inevitable transition from Earth to Heaven.

Then Jesus, this remarkable man, we learn, was just that – a man. He was never nailed to a cross and he never was son of a carpenter. He was not the son of a god either – a reminder, perhaps, in all fairness, that he never said he was. That was an appellation awarded by others much later on after his death.

Here, too, we can dismiss the ideas that Jesus had children by Mary Magdalene or anyone else. The Da Vinci Code novels notwithstanding, that whole idea is fictitious. So is the theory that he was decapitated and his mummified head is still kept secretly in the possession of the Knights Templar. Interestingly though, as we have read, it was his hands that were cut off and for a very special reason. Apart from those, he was buried intact, and he still, to this day, lies in his original and as yet undiscovered tomb in Jerusalem.

These and numerous other distorted memories, false teachings, manipulated exaggerations and downright daft human embellishments of the truth are mentioned at some length in this book. As has often been shrewdly pointed out, old myths never die; they just become embedded in textbooks, such as encyclopaedias, the Bible and learned works of all kinds. The myths of yesterday gradually become the accepted truths of today. In reality they are, of course, and nevertheless remain, still mere myths.

At times – and to some – it seems as if this book came about by accident or pure coincidence. For sure that's what I thought… at the start. As time has passed, however, both the scientifically minded and the more 'spiritually' inclined amongst us have begun to wonder if it was a matter of coincidence after all. Or might it not have been a project that truly had been instigated and influenced by entirely non-human agencies? This is a question likely to recur time and again in the mind of every reader. Is it true? Is it genuine? Is it believable?

When humans die, do they, in fact, become earth spirits, children of God, and, do they, as the spirits tell us, then move to Heaven, where they live happily and forever and have, as their duties, the caring for their descendants still on Earth? And is it sure that reincarnation happens in certain circumstances and it is certain that we will again meet our erstwhile loved-ones in Heaven and stay with them always? This is the message of comfort the book hopes to offer on behalf of its guiding spirits. Most would like it to be true. But then, if wishes were horses…

So there is a crucial choice to be made. Has the author just dreamed this up? That is possible yet with his quiet, successful business and personal life well known to all, it seems a long option. And what about Wilf? He is a quiet, gentle man more at home in his garden, or with his three dogs, or pottering about on his boat. These are two happy, contented, well-adjusted unassuming, semi-retired chaps, gentle men with a myriad of friends who care for and trust them. They certainly come over as rather bewildered by what has happened to them. They appear to take their imposed duties very seriously indeed and have put countless hours into the effort of producing this book.

What, then, are we to do now if we are to follow the lessons of the spirit world? They tell us there are several things needing immediate attention. First, the unbalanced carbon exchange must be curbed. We must attempt to prevent the destruction of the rain forests; they have an important function to help soak up the carbon dioxide.

We must also stop taking oil out of the ground; the spirits are very worried that this is disturbing the delicate weight balance of the Earth. This is also a contributing factor to the Earth's problems.

We, the human race, must find a way to solve the problems swiftly or be prepared to suffer the consequences. Hopefully, with this advanced warning, it will give us all the opportunity and impetus to work together to try and solve the problem before it is too late.

Here, at the end, then, we are the faced with three options. One can disbelieve everything and enjoy the comforts of unbelief or one can adhere to the old religious dicta. Lastly, one can open the mind to new thoughts and ideas. 'Which of these choices sounds the most logical?' we must ask. 'Which sounds more sensible?' Considering the balance of all probabilities, which sounds nearer to the truth?

As I interpret it, several very significant, useful and, above all, deeply comforting facts emerge from the content of this book, which is all spirit-sourced data. No wonder that despite my education and erstwhile convictions, I have so much enjoyed working on the book and learning from its sources.

The four predominant spiritual themes which run through the book are first that death, as we normally think of it being the end of life, simply does not happen. There is no reason whatsoever to be afraid of it. It is not the end of you, but rather the beginning of your spiritual life. Death is an episode of promotion in a continuing life.

Second, we certainly do get to see and be with our loved ones again. Better than that, if we have had a long, happy and loving relationship with another person, the option to meet again and then to remain with each other forever is open to all.

Third, formal religions are largely nonsense-based. There is, therefore, no longer any reason for them to cause dissent, hatred or bloodshed. Furthermore, concerns over eternal punishments for long-past transgressions are unwarranted. There are no such things as days of judgement.

Lastly, but absolutely not least, life truly is eternal and there really is a happy and welcoming afterlife. No one is really dead, they say, while there is anyone still alive who remembers them. Now, perhaps, we see that there is more to it even than that. In one way or another, life really is eternal. Who could ask for anything more?

In the end, it is for you to read, ponder and decide. I can't tell you what to think, but I can tell you what to think about. Each reader must decide this for him or herself. One thing only do I recommend as editor, and I repeat it exactly as our author said at the start, before you kill the messenger, consider the message…